THE BELIEVER'S MANDATE

THE BELIEVER'S MANDATE

Why are we here?

R.C. SMITH

XULON PRESS

Xulon Press
2301 Lucien Way #415
Maitland, FL 32751
407.339.4217
www.xulonpress.com

© 2018 by R.C. SMITH

All rights reserved solely by the author. The author guarantees all contents are original and do not infringe upon the legal rights of any other person or work. No part of this book may be reproduced in any form without the permission of the author. The views expressed in this book are not necessarily those of the publisher.

Scripture quotations taken from the Amplified Bible (AMP). Copyright © 1954, 1958, 1962, 1964, 1965, 1987 by The Lockman Foundation. Used by permission. All rights reserved.

Scripture quotations taken from the King James Version (KJV) – *public domain*.

Scripture quotations taken from the Holy Bible, New Living Translation (NLT). Copyright ©1996, 2004, 2007 by Tyndale House Foundation. Used by permission of Tyndale House Publishers, Inc.

Scripture quotations taken from The Message (MSG). Copyright © 1993, 1994, 1995, 1996, 2000, 2001, 2002. Used by permission of NavPress Publishing Group. Used by permission. All rights reserved.

Scripture quotations taken from the Holy Bible, Modern English Version (MEV). Copyright © 2014 by Military Bible Association. Published and distributed by Charisma House. All rights reserved.

Printed in the United States of America.

ISBN-13: 9781545635421

Table of Contents

Introduction ix
The personal testimony of the Author vii
Chapter one – The Holy One equals Three. 1
Chapter two – Me, myself, and I. 6
Chapter three - Prophetic patterns. 16
Chapter four – The trinity pattern. 23
Chapter five – The Master's key. 42
Chapter six – God's will.. 71
Chapter seven – Love.. 81
Chapter eight – What about the rich guy? 93
Chapter nine – Money or mammon. 115
Chapter ten – No lack.. 134
Chapter eleven – Go, make disciples. 172
Chapter twelve – Do what He did.. 186
Chapter thirteen – Follow the pattern.. 220
Chapter fourteen – Authority crisis.. 228
Chapter fifteen – Enemies of the cross. 237
Chapter sixteen – Perilous times are here. 260
Chapter seventeen – Sin in the camp! 267
Chapter eighteen – The American dream. 285
Chapter nineteen – How to receive God's blessings. . . 300
Chapter twenty – The Name above all names. 312

Introduction

Since the beginning of creation, all mankind has longed for the answer to this soul-searching question: Why am I here? Each one of us has pondered this question at some point along our journey through life. Many times, we find ourselves asking this question in the middle of some conflict or crisis in our lives, such as when we experience a significant loss or a forced change in our lives due to overwhelming circumstances that many times seem so randomly cruel and certainly unwelcome, to say the least.

Perhaps you are at that place right now? Maybe you find yourself again at a crossroad in your life's journey where you know that the next decision or series of decisions that you make will alter your life forever. Well, that is a good place to be. What did you say, a good place? Yes, this is a good place because if you are asking yourself What am I gonna do? or Which way do

I go? or How am I ever going to survive this? then you are at a good place, however; we all need some help to see and understand why we find ourselves at that place again. And it really does not matter what your crisis is: physical, financial, emotional, or spiritual; you will find the answers you are seeking in this book.

Because you have selected this book and have begun to read it, I am going to assume that you are a believer in Jesus Christ, and at some level you already know that God exists and that He is our heavenly Father and the Creator of all things, and that you have some measure of spiritual awareness at this point in your life, and that the Bible is God's inspired message to all of us. However, you also have come to know that there must be more to this quest we call life. I want to encourage you to please stay engaged to the end of this study of, and the search for the Truth. If you do, you shall discover there is real hope, real help, and that you have a very bright future indeed.

It is imperative that we come into agreement on one foundational stone of truth before we proceed. We do not change the Truth, instead the Truth changes us. Therefore, we must agree that the cornerstone of our life foundation is the Word of God and that the Word is the only Way to the Truth and real Life. The Holy

Introduction

Bible is our instruction manual for life, and we must agree on this and make the quality decision to commit ourselves to seeking the Truth.

We must tell you now the reason why it is of such vital importance that we come into agreement 'that the Bible is the Truth' is because we will be referencing from the Scriptures extensively throughout this book, and if you do not believe the Word of God is the Truth, then you won't get much out of this study because no one should care what we think, or what our opinions are.

Therefore, we shall endeavor to establish every precept and principle by, through, and in total alignment with the Truth, which is God's eternal Word; and the plumb line for our life. As our beginning point, the Gospel writer John wrote under the unction of the Holy Spirit the following revelatory Truth about Jesus Christ:

In the beginning was the Word, and the Word was with God, and the Word was God. He was in the beginning with God. All things were created through Him, and without Him nothing was created that was created. In Him was life, and the life was the light of mankind. The light shines in darkness, but the darkness has not overcome it. The Word became flesh and dwelt among us, and we saw His glory, the glory as the only Son of the Father, full of grace and truth. John 1:1-5,14 MEV

And Jesus said to him, I am the way, the truth, and the life. No one comes to the Father except through Me. John 14:6 MEV And Jesus said Heaven and earth will pass away, but My words will not pass away. Mark 13:31 MEV

So, simply stated in very straightforward terms, the living Word of God is Jesus in print; and from this foundational Truth we shall begin to build. We now welcome you to the genesis of our search of the Truth for the comprehensive answer to the incredibly important question: Why are we here?

However, before we launch into the meat of the teaching, I thought you might want to know a bit about who I am, and from where did I come, and why should anyone be interested in reading this book. So, as a way of introducing myself to you, here is a portion of my journey of discovering the Believer's Mandate and why we are here.

The personal testimony of the Author

I was born into a family living in Lawrence County, in southern Missouri, on the eighteenth day of October of 1963, and we lived in the metropolis of Miller, Missouri, with a population of nearly six hundred individuals. (It has just about seven hundred now, almost six decades later) I was the youngest of four children born to Mr. and Mrs. Clifford Hatridge. My given name at birth was Clifford Robert Hatridge. (my family called me Robbie) the oldest was my sister, then second was my brother, and third was another sister, then me. I understand we were born approximately twenty months apart from one another.

When I was about three years of age we were living in an old house in Miller and it caught fire and burned to the ground. That fire was a total loss. We then moved into a trailer house and after a short while, it caught fire. I was in the bathroom and my mother came into the burning trailer home to save me and she threw me out of a window into the yard.

About that time, something exploded (we believe it was the gas hot water heater) and I stood there in the yard and listened to my mother burn to death. We then went to stay with other relatives that lived in the area. Apparently, all of this was more than our father could deal with and he took off leaving us kids to fend for ourselves. He drove a truck to earn a living, and I have been told that a few years later he was killed in some sort of traffic accident.

All of this was overwhelming and too much for the remaining family to cope with. No one wanted me or my siblings, so; we were all separated and became wards of the State, I guess. I didn't know where my brother and sisters were, and I was sent to an orphanage. I don't remember much about all of this except everyone was crying and screaming all the time. It was awful. My little legs were crooked at birth, and I had to wear braces on my legs that attached to a wide belt that went around my waist and extended down and attached to special shoes. I tell you, I must have been a sight.

The Personal Testimony Of The Author

In my short life, I had lost everything except the clothes I had covering my body and those braces on my legs. In a short span of time, we had two houses burn, my mother was killed, my father was gone, and I was rejected by all my aunts, uncles, grandparents, and all the extended family that lived in the area, and I was separated from my brother and sisters. I was alone. I was absolutely alone in this world. I had even lost my name.

In the State of Missouri at that time, when a child is put up for adoption, all your previous records are destroyed. They called me Robbie because like a stray dog at the pound, I would respond to that, but; if you are adopted by someone, they can and do give you a new name and a new birth certificate is issued stating your new name, along with the names of your new legal parents. I find it interesting when others talk about "losing it all" when in-fact, most people really do not have a clue about what it is like to truly lose everything you have even known.

I really don't remember how long I was at this terrible place full of screaming and bawling kids, but; I was adopted by a family that lived in the Ozark Mountains of southern Missouri. I recall these strangers showing-up one day at the place I was being held like a refugee, and I was sitting on the floor with my back against a wall, because there wasn't any place to sit. Here I was, a very broken, scared, little boy without a living soul in this world, sitting there on the floor, with every worldly possession on my body, with these braces on my legs, and holes worn through the bottoms of both of my special shoes. Why would anyone want to adopt such an ugly, broken, and thrown away little boy as me? I truly know beyond doubt that as it is written in Psalm 68:5 God Almighty literally becomes A Father of the fatherless but, more about that revelation later.

One day, into the room walked these strange people and I was told that I must go with them, so; I went. (like I had some choice in the matter.) We rode in this old green Chevy pick-up truck for some time and arrived at this four-room cabin built down in a holler, next to a spring of water coming out of the bottom of the mountain. There was no indoor plumbing, but; each room had a light bulb in the center of the room. We drank from the spring and there was an outhouse on the end of an old broken-down chicken coop. I was informed that *We are your parents now and this is your home.* I guess you might say that I really didn't believe this was my home.

The Personal Testimony Of The Author

Wow was I scared. I didn't eat, drink, or speak for eleven days. My new guardians tried to feed me all the stuff a kid is supposed to like, but; I didn't want anything. I was suffering with a broken heart and a crushed spirit. I really think I would have preferred to just drift off to sleep and never woke-up again.

I was so alone. Who are these people? Where am I? Why am I here? How long do I have to stay here? Where is my real family? Well, on the twelfth day my new mother had cooked a pot of brown beans with cornbread and fried taters. I am not sure if I just got so hungry that I began to eat, or; if beans and cornbread was familiar food to me, but; I ate, and I ate, and I ate some more. My mother tells this story through tears as she says *The day before, we thought 'he is surely going to starve to death'; but now we thought 'he is gonna bust.'* It is interesting that beans, cornbread, and fried potatoes are still one of my favorite meals, to this very day.

Not long after my parents brought me to their cabin, there was an accident. (This incident was my own fault) I was struck on top of the head, knocked out, and split my head open. I recall coming to myself at the doctor's office and being aware that a man was stitching up the wound on my head. You know a four-year-old child's reasoning is not very good, and I know it sounds stupid now, but; I thought that my new parents didn't want me either, just like the rest of my family; and now they had tried to kill me. I was alone. I was so terribly alone.

We went back to the cabin and for a long time during the night hours, I would get out of my bed, and crawl under it, and watch. I reckoned they would come to kill me in my sleep. I reasoned they would come in the dark and wouldn't find me in the bed and just maybe I would have a chance to escape and run away. Right here is a good place to say that my adoptive parents were and are wonderful people (Dad was promoted to heaven on April 10, 2015) and they were good to me, but; I realize now that I don't think they had any idea how broken and emotionally damaged I was, or what to do with me. It certainly was not their fault that I was a very wounded and broken little boy, and I believe they did all they knew to do to try and help me heal.

Well, all this loss and trauma in my short life had trained me to be very suspicious of people and fiercely independent. That is not necessarily a good thing, but; it is how I learned to cope and protect myself. My folks had adopted another baby when he was just six weeks

The Personal Testimony Of The Author

old a couple years before they adopted me, and he was about fourteen months older than I. We did not get along, and our issues were mostly my fault. What was growing and developing in me was a distrust of everyone. I had been so wounded that my defense and coping mechanism was to not allow anyone or anything to get close physically, emotionally, or any other way.

I simply would not allow myself to get attached to anything or anybody. I truly believe that subconsciously I thought if I got close or attached to someone or something, it would be killed or taken away, and I just couldn't stand any more loss. I spent as much time outside and alone as I possibly could and away from people. As I said earlier, we lived down in a holler of the Ozark Mountains at the end of a dead-end road that still had grass growing down the middle of the two tracks. We lived in the sticks, and I loved it. My favorite spots are still the wild and unspoiled places my heavenly Father has made.

Now that you have an idea of my early years and the damage that was done to my young life and soul, I will skip a lot of detail and time in my story and fast-forward a bit.

We attended a little country church and I went to the altar one spring Sunday morning when I was about

11 years old, and ask Jesus to come into my life, and a few days later I was baptized in a small rock bottom stream called Petelo creek, down in the Ozark hills. I can tell you that if I had died after that, I know I would have gone to heaven, but; I still had a lot of wounds and emotional damage in my life and simply stated, I suffered from a broken heart.

I didn't like school and I all my thoughts were about escaping. I just had to get away. Again, I want to say that my folks were very good to me, but; I had never allowed myself to get attached to them, or the brother I was raised with, or with anyone else for that matter. I basically did not trust anyone. I just needed to get old enough to fend for myself and leave, and I did leave when I was seventeen years old. I worked as much as I could, mostly farm labor, until I turned eighteen.

Once I was a legal adult, I got a job as a construction laborer. I didn't know anything, but; I worked hard and paid attention and advanced quickly. The place that I worked at had a young lady that took phone orders for building materials and wrote the delivery and/or installation orders. By this time, I was lead man on the crews and thus I interacted with this young lady daily. I liked her, and she seemed to like me, so; I asked her for a date.

The Personal Testimony Of The Author

She was a farm girl, the youngest of three, and most of her family was in the farming business. They were devout church goers and I really thought that we were equally yoked. If anything, I thought she and her family were all much better people than me. Well, I let down my guard for the first time in my life and let her get closer than anyone I had ever known in my life. We got married, purchased a mobile home, and placed it on the family farm, near the rest of her kinfolk: mom and dad, siblings, and grandparents. I worked at my day job at the construction company along with my wife, and then I helped on the farm in the evenings and weekends, and we all went to church as a family unit. I was completely clueless and thought everything was just going great. Woe, was I one ignorant hick.

Well, this young lady and I were married almost a year, and we were driving home one Sunday after church, and my young bride announces to me as I drove along *I don't want to be married anymore, I want a divorce.* I literally just about crashed the vehicle. I was utterly shocked and devastated just as anyone might be that gets blindsided by this sort of news, however; for me it was even worse because for the first time in my life I had let down my defense system and let someone in to my perimeter and now she has rejected me. I had to leave my home because it was on her families' property, and her family that I had grown fond of all rejected me too. On top of all that I had to go to work every day and not just see her, but; I had to interact with her and communicate with her every day. This was just more than I could take.

Here I was twenty-one years old and without a home, completely rejected again, and I simply could not continue to work at this place and endure interaction with her every day. My absolute worst fears had come true again! I had lost it all again! I was absolutely devastated.

I did not know what to do or where to go. I couldn't eat, I couldn't sleep. I was totally broken, and all my old soul-wounds were ripped open again. How could these good church people (her family) turn on me and behave so dreadful and nasty? How could all this be my fault? I was good to this young woman and we didn't fight or fuss, but she offered no answers except to say will you just go away. I thought everything was awesome. What happened? What in the world did I do wrong? It must be that they just hate me. I guess I can't blame them, because I wasn't really sure if I liked me either. Why did I let my guard down? All of this just reconfirmed the facts: I am unwanted, unlovable, and absolutely nobody can be trusted. When am I gonna quit making that mistake?

I was so distraught and in such deep despair that I did not want to go on living. What is the use? I am doomed. I was taught that God hates divorce, so; He obviously must hate me too. I am all alone and no one can be trusted, and there is just no hope. So, late one night after I had drove around on the country back roads most of the night drinking beer, wallowing in self-pity and despair, I just could not see any hope for any real happiness going forward, so; I decided I would drive down to the place in the hills where I grew-up and take a walk deep into the woods, just like I would when I was a boy, and put a bullet in my brain. Eventually someone would see the buzzards and find my carcass after a few days, but; who cares. I was unwanted, unloved, and totally alone in this world. It is obvious that everyone hated me; including God, so; why go on?

A voice inside my head was screaming, *You're right! There is no hope! Go ahead, do it now!*

There is really nothing extraordinary about my story up to this point. Yeah, it's sad, but; there are lots of people in this world that have had it much worse than me. But, this supernatural event that happened next,

I have shared with very few people over the years, not even my parents until many years later, but; it really happened just this way.

My folks that adopted me pastured some beef cattle on their property and of course my brother and I had daily chores to do and we put up hay every summer to feed during the winter, and we had other livestock too. Well, after my brother got married and moved away and I did the same thing, the folks kept the cattle to graze the place. So, here's the scene: It was about 2:30 AM and I am stumbling along as I pass through this cow pasture, half drunk on beer, with a .44 caliber revolver in my hand, heading for the deep woods to blow a hole in my head.

You know, that seems like the thing to do if all hope is lost. I knew where I was going because I had escaped there a thousand times to get away from everyone. This was my secret place that I would retreat to. This is where I would go to talk to God, but; I wasn't sure He ever heard me, and I was certain He had better things to do than listen to the likes of me. Why would He? I am worthless, unlovable, unwanted by everyone, and in the process of becoming divorced, and we know God hates that!

I was so alone.

The Personal Testimony Of The Author

As I stumbled along, I was crying-out to this awesome God that I was sure had more important things to tend to than this worthless broken vessel that was a total failure as a son, brother, friend, husband, and human being, and now headed for divorce. I knew that the Bible said that God hated divorce, so; I thought I was headed for hell anyway, so; I thought, what's the use? Why should I continue to hurt and suffer any longer? I know this sounds stupid, but; this is where I was at, and the enemy was right there agreeing with every word. I had received little or no teaching in our denominational church, and I was still an infant spiritually speaking. But, hold on and let me tell you what happened next.

As I was stumbling along to my doom, crying out to God that I was truly sorry that I was so worthless, unlovable, and had brought so much trouble and pain into other people's lives; something very strange happened as I was trekking across this cow pasture. As I said earlier, it was about 2:30 or 3:00 in the morning, and as I was weeping and squalling, I heard something behind me. I turned to look, thinking it might have been some sort of a wild animal; and I noticed that my folks' cattle were now following me.

I recall thinking that is weird, cattle don't wander around in the middle of the night, and about that time the whole herd broke into a sprint, and they were running directly at me! I had never seen anything like this before, so; alarmed, I took off running too. I thought these crazy cows want me dead too! But, as this herd of cows caught up with me, they surrounded me, and started slowing down and squeezing together until I was captured and physically stopped and was being held in place by these wacko cows. I was yelling and punching and kicking these cows with everything I had in me, but; they were not budging. In fact, the ones closest to me began licking me like a dog. These cows had literally arrested me in the middle of this pasture at 3:00 in the morning. Then, as on some silent signal, they all just laid down and went to sleep, the whole herd, the young and old were all sound asleep. There wasn't a sound at that moment and the silence was deafening. I just stood there in total shock and awe. I had never seen or heard of cattle behaving like this before. I was completely dumbfounded. I knew this had to be the handiwork of God. There was not any natural explanation, this was supernatural.

Well, I fell to my knees and wept there with the cows until I couldn't weep anymore, and I felt like the weight of the world was lifted off me, and I was at peace inside. There was still a lot of negative stuff going on in my life, but; I then knew that God cared enough about me that He sent a herd of dumb ole' cows to stop me from killing myself. God is so awesome; He knows where we are and just what we need no matter what is going on, or how incredibly ignorant we may be. The message I received from those cows that night was more effective for me at that moment than ten preachers would have been. Praise God! It was now at this point that I began to wonder if God didn't have something better for me, and I just might have something to look forward to in the future. Hope was restored. Could I dare to dream again?

I resigned by job at the place where I was working, and with the Lord's help; I got a better job and moved to another town hours away. I was now selling building materials and subcontracting portions of the work on residential and some small commercial construction projects. That led to increasingly better opportunities. I accepted a position with a large commercial General Contractor and was a project manager for them. I was doing well in my work life, but; I couldn't say I was doing much for the Lord, but; I had learned that Father God doesn't hate people that get divorced, He hates divorce because of what it does to His people and families.

Seven years had come and gone, and I had some female friends that I had dating relationships with, but; they all were doomed to fail because I would not let them get close or personal. If they spoke of commitment or any mention of marriage, I would put a quick end to that relationship, until one day I was leaving my office that was located within a large office complex in the downtown area of the city where I was living and working, when this young woman walking into her place of employment caught my eye. Well, shortly thereafter we met, went on a date and I learned that she was a preacher's daughter, but; tragically her father had died suddenly when she was twelve years of age. I remember thinking that we had a lot in common, and her family were all good church folk too. Again, if anything they all were better people than me. Well, I fell for this one and thought that we understood one another and had many similar life experiences. We were engaged and got married. She worked for a major Real Estate brokerage firm in our city, and I had an acceptable position with a significant commercial contractor in the area and life was good and getting better, so I thought.

The Personal Testimony Of The Author

Well, to fast forward a bit here, I had an opportunity to buy-in to an established commercial contracting business and I pursued it. We had been married now a little over six years and had two children. I kept building the business and she was a stay at home mom. Years went by and the business grew and so did our income. At this time, we had been married fifteen years, the children were thriving, and we were attending a local church. We had just finished building a large new home and we had all the toys.

The contracting business was busy, and I had started a land development company as well. We had formed many different partnerships developing, buying, selling, building, and leasing properties. I was very, very busy and with all these diverse deals, partners, projects, and banking relationships, the business was very complex, but; it looked like there was no end to the growth and expansion in the future. I was building a kingdom and as they say, "we were on a roll" until Monday evening, the twelfth day of November of 2007. That day I came home in the evening after work as was typical and walked into our big house and no one was there. I found a small note on the counter in the kitchen that simply said in so many words that my spouse had left, took the children, and had filed for divorce, and she was quite emphatic that I was not to come looking for her because it was over.

Remarkably, my business partners and I had just spent the last eighteen months working with estate planning lawyers crafting all sorts of documents like buy/sell agreements, wills, etc. carefully defining how to direct all these various closing transactions for the businesses, partnerships, land deals, and developments, should one of the principal partners die, become disabled, or get divorced. I never dreamed it would be me that would trigger these agreements and various documents that were just completed, fully executed, and in full force.

All of these things were occurring at the last quarter of 2007 and entering 2008. This was categorically one of the worst times in history to be in the construction and land development business. My head still spins in awe to this day trying to figure out exactly what all happened. It was the perfect storm. I and my various partners were all optimistically overleveraged and deep in debt on these various projects. We were shifting and leveraging money from one deal to the next deal and working very hard and every angle in our attempts to keep it all afloat. My estranged spouse did not understand the business and certainly didn't understand the details of the various deals, projects, and partnerships, but; she was sure everybody was trying to cheat her. It was a huge mess. Long story short, within about forty days I did not have a home, I did not have a business, I did not have a job, I did not have any income, I did not have any partnerships, I did not have a friend, and I did not have my family. I was all alone…. Again.

As recorded in Job 3:25-26 MEV: For the thing which I greatly feared has happened to me, and that which I dreaded has come to me. I am not at peace; I have no quiet, I cannot rest, and turmoil has come. Just like Job, my worst fears had come upon me again and I did not have any peace. I have never been a greedy person, and despite popular opinion; I was not building this so-called kingdom for the sake of the money. No, I was building this supposed kingdom thinking foolishly that if I could just make enough money and have enough stuff, then I wouldn't be alone, and people will appreciate me and value me somehow. I was wrong. I crashed very hard. There are many things I could say about these events and all the things that happened, but; the bottom line is that my world, and the walls of my contrived kingdom; came crashing down around me again, and I was all alone.

It was wintertime and cold and snowy in the first part of January 2008, and I was living in an empty house that was owned, by this time; a now ex-friend and ex-business partner. He was in the process of rezoning the property to commercial and had plans to tear it down when that process was completed, but; simply out of the goodness of his heart, he allowed me to stay there at a reasonable cost. I didn't deserve that favorable treatment from him because I had been the source of much distress and angst for him, and for my other business partners as well; for which I deeply regret.

I did not have a job and no prospect for one at the time. I was fighting the divorce and struggling with numerous other legal issues with ex-partners, banks, etc., etc. It was wintertime and cloudy inside and outside, and I was all alone. What a mess I had made. What a catastrophe. I did not know what to do, or where to go. I was at the end of myself. I was at the end of my rope and nothing but a dark pit below me. Why did this pattern keep happening over and over?

It was now Monday evening, and a very humble and godly man at church the day before had loaned me a book, and I just knew I had to read it. This book was written by a gentleman with at least two doctorate degrees and had several acronyms after his name. But more importantly, this book's author was a devout follower of Jesus Christ.

This man of God was writing about how to receive healing from painful emotions and the deep wounds in our souls, that many individuals suffer from throughout their whole lives. He wrote about how traumas from our past, especially those traumatic events occurring in our early childhood; will profoundly affect and arrest our development if we do not receive deep healing in our emotions and souls. I was receiving revelation that night as I read this book that I was wounded and broken, and just as the Word of God instructs: Keep your heart with all diligence, for out of it are the issues of life. Proverbs 4:23 MEV

The "issues" of my life were an absolute mess because I was suffering from a broken heart, and my brokenness had adversely affected every aspect of my life. These damaged places in my soul had negatively impacted every relationship throughout my entire lifetime, and now I can clearly see the problem. I was the walking wounded. I was hurt, and I was the problem. I was deeply traumatized and nothing and nobody could touch or heal the broken places in my soul, except Jesus Christ.

The Believer's Mandate

I want to share with you now what this whole story and this entire book is about. It's all about Jesus. Oh, what a Savior, oh what a Healer, oh what a Way Maker my Jesus is.

It was about midnight that cold winter's night in that old empty house, as I was there alone. I had just finished reading the book that this awesome servant of God had loaned me, and I finally saw the problem, but; more importantly I now had revelation of the solution. I fell to my knees and I cried out to Jesus. I guess you could call this a prayer. I just lifted my voice and said: JESUS! I AM A MESS! I CAN NOT LIVE LIKE THIS ANOTHER DAY! I am asking You Lord to please come now and heal me of all my past hurts and wounds and forgive me for all the wrong I have done. Lord Jesus please heal my broken heart. I do not want to hurt any more, and I will serve You for the rest of my life. Amen.

What happened next still brings me to tears every time I remember, including right now; as I type these words.

In an open vision, I became like a four-year-old child again and I was transported to that hill just outside the city walls of Jerusalem called Calvary. Jesus was there on the cross and I was before him about

The Personal Testimony Of The Author

seven or eight feet away on my knees. From behind me came a hot wind or breath, and I heard my heavenly Father say to me, *son, I love you. This is how much I love you, and you have never been alone.* I was there at the cross with Jesus just a few moments more and then I was back in the old house where I was staying. I was lying down on my back and I could not get up, and I could not move. I was so very heavy, and the ceiling of the room became like a movie screen as my life passed before me rapidly, just like a fast-forwarded video.

It can be difficult to describe and explain spiritual things, but I know I can't do much better than to simply say that Jesus did heart surgery on me that night as He touched and healed those deep wounds in my soul. As the Lord poured out His love on me throughout the night, it was so overwhelming that I could not move, and I could not speak a work in English for quite some time, hours, I believe. I really do not know. It was near midnight when this encounter began, and it was daylight when I could get up and move about again. This close encounter with the Lord has been the most profound event in my life. Every day from that moment to this one right now, I have been experiencing and living a supernatural, Spirit led life! Oh, glory to God!

I wasn't sure what had happened to me. At that point, I hadn't had any teaching about the Holy Spirit, or the baptism of the Holy Ghost and fire. I am surely thankful and grateful that the Lord did not let my ignorance stop Him from healing me, and filling me with His Spirit, and showing me His glory that night. Thank you, Jesus. I love you Lord.

As I have said, from that very moment, everything changed. After that, the Lord led me to go to Nicaragua on a mission trip to build houses for folks there and to minister to the people. That was an amazing trip. I heard the audible voice of God again while there in the city of Managua. Early one morning about 4:00 am, the Holy Spirit woke me and told me to go outside, and I did. As I sat by myself admiring the early morning sky, the Lord spoke to me and said: *son, give your old life a decent burial and move on, because I have places for you to go and things for you to do for Me!* I answered Him: *Yes, Lord*.

During that trip, I met a man in Nicaragua that led to a job opportunity in east Tennessee to be a project manager on a very large commercial development. It was on Father's Day, Sunday June fifteenth, 2008, the Holy Spirit woke me at about 3:00 AM and told me to

The Personal Testimony Of The Author

rise and get my Bible. I did, and He instructed me to open to Isaiah chapter 61 and read, and I did:

The Spirit of the Sovereign Lord is on me, because the Lord has anointed me to preach good news to the poor. He has sent me to bind up the brokenhearted, to proclaim freedom for the captives and release from darkness for the prisoners, to proclaim the year of the Lord's favor and the day of vengeance of our God, to comfort all who mourn, and provide for those who grieve in Zion – to bestow on them a crown of beauty instead of ashes, the oil of gladness instead of mourning, and a garment of praise instead of a spirit of despair. They will be called oaks of righteousness, a planting of the Lord for the display of his splendor. Isaiah 61:1-3 NIV

As I read this passage the Holy Spirit said to me: *This is you, this is what I want you to do.* I now understand that out of our mess comes our message, and this was my call into ministry and this is my life mission. I was there in Sevier County, Tennessee until the Lord said it was time to go in November. From east Tennessee, the Lord led me to Michigan and I relocated there on December eighth in two thousand eight, to accept a suitable position with a company there and to meet my God ordained help mate. I met my beautiful wife Kathy in Michigan (she was a special education teacher for twenty-five years) and we got married on the twentieth day of November in two thousand nine.

About forty days later, on the first of January of two thousand ten, the Holy Spirit spoke to me and said that Kathy and I were to resign our positions, sell and/or give away everything, leave Michigan and our family, and attend Rhema Bible Training College in Broken Arrow, Oklahoma. So, we obeyed.

That was a huge faith adventure. While there, we had testimony after testimony to the Lord's faithfulness and we witnessed many signs, wonders, and miracles. In January of two thousand eleven, after a three day fast, and a very difficult test (being jailed for my testimony for Jesus), the Lord spoke with me about my calling and the office(s) He would eventually place me in. After graduating RBTC on May fourteen of two thousand twelve, the Lord led us to move to Ghana, West Africa and help start a Bible college there, which we did. Then after five months, we were led to return to the States and the Lord had Kathy begin teaching special needs children again. The Holy Spirit led me to return to Africa to join an evangelistic team and mobile Bible school operation and we traveled in Zambia and Zimbabwe teaching Pastors and Church lay leaders every day for three weeks before holding large outdoor evangelistic gatherings for five to six days before moving to the next location. We did this repeatedly for the balance of the year.

I returned from that mission to the USA and then started a home group ministry teaching adults the Word of God. At that time, I was studying the Scriptures approximately forty to fifty hours a week and additionally was taking an on-line class learning Biblical Hebrew from the University of Jerusalem. We would then have about eight to ten hours of classroom teaching per week for those hungry for the things of God. This continued for about two and a half years, and in August two thousand sixteen the Lord led us to relocate to the southeast for our new mission there that He has called *Tree of Life International*, to bring healing to the Nations, (based on Revelation 22:2). Amen.

I am leaving out many extraordinary signs, wonders, miracles, and healings that the Lord has done in us, for us, and working through us; confirming His Word and using our hands and feet to minister to His people. The Lord is good, and He has blessed us, and continues to bless Kathy and me greatly. The Lord has taught us many things and we are living the life of faith, day by day, walking out His plans and purposes with Him. Our heavenly Father truly does become the *Father to the fatherless*, in every way, and He is forever faithful.

The Lord has been stirring us about doing a new thing, and we shall wait on Him to see what's next. Stay tuned! Thank you for your time, and may the Lord richly bless you.

After more than twenty-five years in the construction industry, and a very dramatic encounter with the Lord, I answered the call and transitioned into ministry full time. Following a year of attending a formal Bible school while still in Michigan in two thousand nine, we then attended Rhema Bible Training College full time from the late summer of two thousand ten till the spring of two thousand twelve. Since that season, we have continued to passionately preach, teach, and study the Word of God and intend to remain devoted, teachable students of God's Word for the rest of our lives and eternity. If we have learned anything it is this: We can do nothing worthwhile apart from Him. Our Teacher, the Holy Spirit; has revealed to us many Truths within the written Word and the purpose of this book and the ministry website is to be a teaching ministry and to make available to all the revelations that the Holy Spirit has shown us over the years through our writings, teachings, and audio/video files. I pray that you will receive a spirit of wisdom and revelation as you pursue the things of God. Amen

I love my best friend Jesus, and I just can't get over all the good things He has done for me. Therefore, I shall serve Him the rest of my days, and in the age to come, and for all eternity. Hallelujah!

In His service,

R.C. Smith, *bond-servant* of Jesus Christ

Tree of Life International
11631 Sonoma Road
Battle Creek, MI 49015
toil.rcsmith@gmail.com
treeoflifeinternational.net

Tree of Life International is an outreach missions ministry, with the God given mandate to organize gatherings in churches, arenas, stadiums, and other secular locations in the United States and other Nations of the world as the Lord leads, for the expressed purpose of teaching and preaching the Good News message that Jesus Christ is alive, and Jesus heals, and Jesus saves, and Jesus delivers, and He is coming again

The Believer's Mandate

soon to establish the Kingdom age. Jesus Christ is the same yesterday, and today, and forevermore! Amen.

Please join in with us as we walk with Jesus on the journey to our eternal home and as we endeavor to take many souls with us.

Then He said to His disciples, The harvest truly is plentiful, but the laborers are few. Therefore, pray to the Lord of the harvest, that He will send out laborers into His harvest. Matthew 9:37-38 MEV

CHAPTER ONE

The Holy One equals Three

Foundational Truth: We are created beings, made in the image and likeness of God our Creator.

In the beginning God created the heavens and the earth. The earth was formless and void, darkness was over the surface of the deep, and the Spirit of God was moving over the surface of the water. Genesis 1:1-2 MEV

Here in the very first passage of Scripture in the Bible, we see established the Godhead: The Father, Son, and Holy Spirit; or the Holy Trinity. The Old Covenant Scriptures were mostly written in the Hebrew language (a small portion of the Old Testament was written in Aramaic) and many times we can profit significantly from returning to the original text and language to receive greater revelation of exactly what

God is revealing to us, and in this case; the English word God, which is transliterated from Hebrew to English, from the Hebrew word *Elohim*. (Hebrew hint: whenever you see the "im" on the end of a word, it is almost always masculine plural)

The most literal translation of *Elohim* means "Creators" plural, and of course we also see here clearly in this passage in verse two, the Holy Spirit. As an interesting side note, we know the Bible was inspired by God: Father, Son and Holy Spirit, and the original Scriptures were composed in three languages Hebrew, Aramaic, & Greek, and the Gospel of John begins with In the beginning was the Word, and the Word was with God, and the Word was God. clearly making the distinct reference to Genesis 1:1.

So, we see revealed that Elohim, God plural; along with Holy Spirit, is our Creator. We also know that the Word is, was, and always will be God, and that it was given to us originally in three languages. We will discuss and illustrate with additional Truths in a following chapter how the number three is a perfect number, meaning that is represents a complete, whole unit and representing divine perfection. So, reading on in Genesis chapter one, we see the passage of Scripture that records the creation of man, or Adam; on the sixth and final day of God's work of creation.

God said, Let Us [Father, Son and Holy Spirit] make mankind in Our image, after Our likeness, and let them have complete authority over the fish of the sea, the birds of the air, the [tame] beasts, and over all the earth, and over everything that creeps upon the earth. So God created man in His own image, in the image and likeness of God He created him; male and female He created them. And God blessed them and said to them, Be fruitful, multiply, and fill the earth, and subdue it [using all its vast resources in the service of God and man]; and have dominion over the fish of the sea, the birds of the air, and over every living creature that moves upon the earth. Genesis 1:26-28 AMPC

Elohim - God our Creator, the triune Love, Light, and Life; created mankind in His image and likeness, which means we humans also must certainly be a triune, three-part being.

Beloved, let us love one another, for love is of God, and everyone who loves is born of God and knows God. Any one who does not love does not know God, for God is love. In this way the love of God was revealed to us, that God sent His only begotten Son into the world, that we might live through Him. I John 4:7-9 MEV

And we have come to know and believe the love that God has for us. God is love. Whoever lives in love lives in God, and God in him. I John 4:16 MEV

In Him was life, and the life was the light of mankind. The light shines in darkness, but the darkness has not overcome it. John 1:4-5 MEV

Every good gift and perfect gift is from above and comes down from the Father of lights, with whom is no change or shadow of turning. James 1:17 MEV

This then is the message which we have heard from him and declare to you: God is light, and in Him is no darkness at all. I John 1:5 MEV

And this is the testimony: that God has given us eternal life, and this life is in His Son. Whoever has the Son has life, and whoever does not have the Son of God does not have life. I John 5:11-12 MEV

We all must receive revelation of this incredible Truth in our spirits with the help of the Holy Spirit because in our minds we can't fully understand or comprehend the Godhead with our natural facilities of understanding and accurately grasp that the Holy One is Three.

And we know that the Son of God has come and has given us understanding, so that we may know Him who is true, and we are in Him who is true – His Son Jesus Christ. He is the true God and eternal life. I John 5:20 MEV

We must come to know and believe in the Father, Son, and Holy Spirit. We must know and believe that Father God sent His Son to be manifested in bodily form, anointed by the Holy Spirit; into this fallen world to give us life.

This is the Believer's Mandate.

CHAPTER TWO

Me, myself, and I

Foundational Truth: We are a spirit, we have a soul, and we live in a body, just like Father God our Creator manifest Himself.

We know from our study of the Bible that Father God created Adam and Eve, male and female only, husband and wife, (there is not a third option) He blessed them and commanded them to multiply. We can see that God's plan for the family unit was one adult man joined in the covenant bond of marriage to one adult woman, and thus they would naturally reproduce having offspring, some male and some female. This is God's implicit will for mankind regarding the marriage covenant and sexual relationships, thus multiplying and producing the family unit.

Any other deviation and/or version of this plan is not God's will and therefore is immoral, wrong, confused, and dysfunctional. To be abundantly clear on this point, any other human relationship outside God's original plan is sin and corruption. (We can't move past the opportunity here to speak into this issue of the definition of family because there is widespread confusion in contemporary culture about this clear, fundamental, and unchanging Truth.) We are not saying this behavior is wrong, God Almighty is declaring it!

Okay, lets return to the foundational Truth that Father God is a triune being.

Father God is Spirit:

God is Spirit, and those who worship Him must worship Him in spirit and truth. John 4:24 MEV God is omnipotent, omniscient, and omnipresent, which means He is all-powerful, all-knowing, and ever-present.

God is also infinite, eternal, and immutable, which means He is free from all limitations whatsoever. God is, God was, and God will always be. The Lord God Almighty is unchangeable. He alone is all-knowing, ever-present and without limits. He is the Beginning and the Ending, and Everything in between. He is the First and the Last. God is the great I AM. The Lord God Almighty is Spirit.

Father God has a soul, which is His mind, will, and emotions:

Great is our Lord and great in power; His understanding is without measure. Psalm 147:5 For My thoughts are not your thoughts, nor are your ways My ways, says the Lord. Isaiah 55:8 Therefore pray in this manner: Our Father who is in heaven, hallowed be Your name. Your kingdom come; Your will be done on earth, as it is in heaven. Matthew 6:9-10 For God is the One working in you, both to will and to do His good pleasure. Philippians 2:13 The Lord is a jealous and avenging God; the Lord avenges and is furious. The Lord takes vengeance on His enemies, and He reserves it for His adversaries; the Lord is slow to anger and great in power, and the Lord will in no way acquit the guilty. Nahum 1:2-3 When He had made a whip of cords, He drove them all out of the temple, with the sheep and oxen. He poured out the changers' money and overturned the tables. John 2:15 Jesus wept. John 11:35 MEV

Father God has a body:

For the eyes of the Lord move about on all the earth to strengthen the heart that is completely toward Him. II Chronicles 16:9a Then Moses went up with Aaron, Nadab, and Abihu, and seventy of the elders of Israel, and they saw the God of Israel, and under His feet there was something like a paved work of sapphire stone as clear as the sky itself. He did not lay His hand upon the nobles of the children of Israel. Also they saw God, and they ate and they drank. Exodus 24:9-11 When He had made an end of communing with him on Mount Sinai, He gave Moses the two tablets of stone, written with the finger of God. Exodus 31:18 Then the Lord said, Indeed, there is a place by Me. You must stand on the rock. While My glory passes by, I will put you in a cleft of the rock and will cover you with My hand while I pass by. Then I will take away My hand, and you will see My back, but My face may not be seen. Exodus 33:21-23 But being full of the Holy Spirit, he gazed into heaven and saw the glory of God, and Jesus standing at the right hand of God, and said, Look! I see the heavens opened and the Son of Man standing at the right hand of God. Acts 7:55-56 MEV

Father God created us as triune beings in His image and likeness and placed the man Adam and his wife Eve in the distinct garden that God created within Eden for man to dwell in, and they were naked and unashamed. Have you ever thought about how incredibly perfect this earthly garden had to be for Adam and Eve to live outside twenty-four hours of every day with no clothes, no house and no way to control their environment? They did not get hot, and they didn't get cold, and they were naked yet without being conscious of their nakedness. They did not need nor had want of anything whatsoever within this immaculate paradise created just for man.

We shall submit to you this thought to contemplate. Adam and Eve must have been "covered" by something else. We believe that they were sheltered or clothed by the glory of God. We believe Adam and Eve were clothed with and by light or stated another way; they were surrounded by God's glorious manifest presence. Wow.

Our earthly progenitors, Adam and Eve; were created to be in the constant presence and fellowship with the Creator. Father God wanted a family and God wanted fellowship with His family. Therefore, God created man because He wanted to have sons and daughters that He could pour out His limitless lovingkindness upon and to be loved in return, from our own free will. Our heavenly Father wanted volunteer lovers. God created man in His image as a spirit being, possessing a soul, and placed both spirit and soul, in a body of flesh (that we like to call our earth suit) that was designed to function comfortably and in perfect harmony forever within this ideal environment fashioned by Father God that we know as the Garden of Eden or paradise. So, what happened?

We know from Scripture that within the Garden were many flora and fauna and God commanded man and said that he could freely eat of every tree of the Garden, excluding one tree. That one and only exception was the tree of the knowledge of good and evil, and God said if he did choose to eat of that tree he would surely die. So, we know when our enemy, Satan; manifested as a walking, talking serpent in the Garden, and tempted Eve in three areas defined as the lust of the flesh, lust of the eyes, and the pride of life. (I John 2:15-17) Eve took of the forbidden fruit and ate and gave it to Adam and he ate. The Scriptures teach us that their eyes were opened, and they knew they were naked, and they then took fig leaves and tried to fashion coverings for themselves. They were shamed, worried, self-conscious, discomforted, and fearful and thus strained to hide themselves. What came next? The ole' blame game was conceived as Adam blamed Eve and Eve blamed the deception of the serpent. (Genesis 2:15-3:13)

What an utter disaster. There is much to be said and many lessons within this passage of important

Scripture, but; we would like to remain on the trail of discovery of what happened when Adam and Eve made the free-will choice to believe and heed the words of a talking snake over the words of God Almighty who created Adam and Eve, the tree, and the snake. The first iniquity they were guilty of committing that day wasn't the eating of the fruit. The sin they committed was unbelief, borne out of feelings of discontentment; and as the Garden paradise was corrupted when sin entered the Garden, sin entered all of mankind. But, what exactly had changed then?

God had said to Adam; but of the tree of the knowledge of good and evil you shall not eat, for in the day that you eat from it you will surely die. Genesis 2:17 MEV. However, we know from the Scripture in Genesis 5:5 that after some short span of time following the fall, they were expelled from the Garden of Eden, and Adam lived nine hundred thirty years before his physical body expired and he died naturally.

What we must understand is that man was made by God, in His image and likeness, therefore; Adam was a spiritual being alive unto God, and that he had a soul, and he lived in a body, and Adam was a direct creation of God without sin, flaw, or corruption of any kind. When Adam and Eve disobeyed God's instructions and thus sinned, their spirits died, and you could say their eternal light went out and God had to withdraw His presence from them because a Holy God cannot be in the presence of sin and defilement. So, at that moment when Adam and Eve transgressed, the divine light that had clothed them was withdrawn, thus they could distinguish their nakedness. Sin, shame, anxiety, fear, corruption, deceit, and death entered the world and brought a curse upon the lives of men. This is called the curse of the fall.

So, from that point forward, all of mankind was and is conceived under the curse of the fall and born with a fallen sin nature. So, the net result of Adam and Eves transgression is every human being since Adam are conceived and born spiritually dead and eternally separated from God. Thus, we too must choose between the two trees: the tree of life, or the tree of the knowledge of good and evil, just like Adam and Eve made their choice that day. We each must choose to listen, trust, and obey the words of God Almighty, or believe and follow the words of the father of lies and the enemy of our souls.

Aren't you thankful that God didn't leave us in that hopeless state? No, He did not, and matter of fact; He instigated the greatest rescue plan ever conceived and fully executed in all of history. God Almighty gave and sent His very best, His only begotten Son Jesus; so, we could be reconciled, ransomed, and fully restored back to fellowship with the Father through our belief in Jesus' sinless life, sacrificial death, and resurrection from the grave. By our faith in Jesus' life, death, and resurrection, each one of us can choose to invite Jesus to be our personal Savior, Redeemer, and Lord. Hallelujah.

Now, before we move on in our study, let us do a quick review. We are born in the image and likeness of our earthly parents that passed along the fallen sin nature to us, and we are spirit beings, that have a soul, and we live in our flesh bodies. If we do nothing more than grow up and live out our natural lives the way we choose to live here on earth, eventually our bodies will wear-out and succumb to death of old age, or from the effects of sickness and disease. (The current documented mortality rate is 100%) We all need to understand that life begins at conception in our mother's womb and from that moment of union of the egg and seed, our eternal life begins, and we all have everlasting life from that moment on.

Our spirits and souls are eternal, and when our physical flesh body fails us in death, and returns to the dust of the earth, our spirit and soul will continue to live forever in one of two very real perpetual locations. Those two ultimate and perpetual destinations are heaven above with the Father, Son and Holy Spirit, dwelling in perfect light, love, and peace with the angelic host; or below in the lake of fire consumed by eternal terror, torment, regret and darkness with the devil and his demonic horde.

We all must deliberately choose our eternal destination, and if someone does not make this conscious choice, they have in-fact chosen because the default destination from birth because of our hereditary fallen sin-nature is hell. So, repent and believe, thus making the only wise choice of love, light, and life in Jesus.

This is the Believer's Mandate.

Chapter Three

Prophetic patterns

F oundational Truth: God teaches us through prophetic types, shadows, similitudes, and patterns.

The sum of Your word is truth [the total of the full meaning of all Your individual precepts]; and every one of Your righteous decrees endures forever. Psalm 119:160 AMPC

Thus says the Lord: Stand in the court of the Lord's house [Jeremiah] and speak to all [the people of] the cities of Judah who come to worship in the Lord's house all the words that I command you to speak to them; subtract not a word. Jeremiah 26:2 AMPC

Therefore I testify to you this day that I am innocent of the blood of all men. For I did not keep from declaring to you the whole counsel of God. Acts 20:27-28 MEV

When you begin seeking the Truth, that is dispersed throughout the whole counsel of God, (which means that one must study all of God's Word from Genesis to Revelation), you will begin to see these types, shadows, similitudes, and patterns revealed throughout the Bible, and this three-part triune being pattern created by God is no exception. So, let's have a bit deeper look at some examples of this within the Scriptures, but; first let us hear what God's Word teaches explicitly regarding His patterns.

The thing that has been – it is what will be again, and that which has been done is that which will be done again; and there is nothing new under the sun. Ecclesiastes 1:9 AMPC

That which is now already has been, and that which is to be already has been; and God seeks that which has passed by [so that history repeats itself]. Ecclesiastes 3:15 AMPC

Remember the former things of old, for I am God, and there is no other; I am God, and there is no one like Me, declaring the end from the beginning, and from ancient times the things that are not yet done, saying, My counsel shall stand, and I will do all My good pleasure. Isaiah 46:9-10 MEV

I have also spoken by the prophets, and have multiplied visions, and used similitudes, by the ministry of the prophets. Hosea 12:10 KJV

Someone once said that history is His story, and that is correct. The Bible includes much history, and as we can see that by Divine design, history repeats itself because God is trying to teach us lessons on how to live through His story written down as examples and patterns for us to model our lives after, and hopefully avoid the mistakes made by our forefathers of faith. In this way, the Lord teaches us what the future will bring, and this is what we call prophetic types, shadows, similitudes, and patterns.

Now all these things happened to them for examples. They are written as an admonition to us, upon whom the end of the ages has come. I Corinthians 10:11 MEV

As a primary example of this principal, the Lord commanded Moses to create a tabernacle in the wilderness, patterned exactly after the tabernacle in heaven. Let them make Me a sanctuary that I may dwell among them. According to all that I show you – the pattern of the tabernacle and the pattern of all its furniture – you shall make it just so. Exodus 25:8 MEV They serve in a sanctuary that is an example and a shadow of the heavenly one, as Moses was instructed by God when he was about to make the tabernacle, See that you make all things according to the pattern shown you on the mountain. Hebrews 8:5 MEV

Then we see recorded in the Scriptures how God gives His instructions through the ministry of His angels (Acts 7:53, Galatians 3:19) to Moses on Mount Horeb, all the intricate details about the tabernacle (Exodus 25-31, 35-40) and very precise instructions on how all the different elements of the structure must be made, and all the details about the fabrication of the Ark, fixtures, furniture, garments, ornaments, anointing oil, lamp oil, and altar incense. Each item and every detail are very important to the prophetic meaning and pattern behind the literal elements that were to be used, placed, consumed, or worn while engaged in the daily sacrifices and worship of God Almighty. Every single dimension and detail about the materials and all the individual elements that God commanded Moses to make are symbolic of something important to God, and therefore; very important to us. There have been volumes of good books written about all the various prophetic types, shadows, similitudes, and patterns concealed within the details of the construction and all the prescribed daily activities of the Levites and priests executing their service and worship of God within the tabernacle that are very important and worthy of study. However, for our efforts we will look at just one very clear pattern within the tabernacle of Moses, of its overall design and composition.

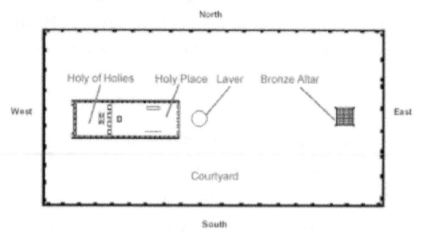

The tabernacle has been called the wilderness church, and as you can see, it was designed, fabricated, and erected to create three principal defined areas or components: The Courtyard, the Holy Place and the Holy of Holies. The tabernacle at-large and these three specifically compartmentalized areas are symbolic of the Church. Therefore, the tabernacle is a pattern of us, as we are the church, or the temple of the living God, here on earth.

Do you not know that you are the temple of God, and that the Spirit of God dwells in you? If anyone defiles the temple of God, God will destroy him. For the temple of God is holy. And you are His temple. I Corinthians 3:16-17 MEV

What? Do you not know that your body is the temple of the Holy Spirit, who is in you, whom you have received from God, and that you are not your own? You were bought with a price. Therefore glorify God in your body and in your spirit, which are God's. I Corinthians 6:19-20 MEV

What agreement has the temple of God with idols? For you are the temple of the living God. As God has said: I will live in them and walk in them. I will be their God, and they shall be My people. Therefore, Come out from among them and be separate, says the Lord. Do not touch what is unclean, and I will receive you. I will be a Father to you, and you shall be My sons and daughters, says the Lord Almighty. II Corinthians 6:16-18 MEV

These three compartments of the tabernacle are a type, shadow, and pattern of our triune being. The Courtyard is symbolic of our body, and the Holy Place is symbolic of our soul, and the Holy of Holies is symbolic of our spirit. Again, many good books have expounded on all the symbolism of the tabernacle, but; what we need to comprehend is that God uses types, shadows, and patterns to establish His Truths, and we can clearly see revealed in this example, the triune construction pattern that is a similitude of us human beings that our Master fashioned. God Almighty created us as spirit beings, that have souls, and we dwell in physical bodies.

Now, we shall advance and study a significantly more complex example of this God fashioned three-part triune similitude and pattern that has a much greater sweep throughout all post-flood human history.

God Almighty created mankind us in His image and likeness, so He might have a large family that would willingly love and worship Him.

And Jesus answered him, Get behind Me, Satan! For it is written, You shall worship the Lord your God, and Him only shall you serve. Luke 4:8 MEV

This is the Believer's Mandate.

Chapter Four

The trinity pattern

Foundational Truth: The three sons of Noah repopulated the entire earth after the flood and they represent a type, shadow, similitude, and pattern of the three-part triune composition of all mankind, created in the image of our heavenly Father.

Noah, in the tenth generation from Adam, when wickedness, evil, and corruption had so filled the earth and men's hearts and imaginations to the point that God Almighty had to bring the cleansing flood upon all the earth. Then after the great floodwaters that had covered the earth had receded: Then God spoke to Noah, saying, Go out of the ark, you and your wife, and your sons and your sons' wives with you. Genesis 8:15-16 MEV Then God blessed Noah and his sons and said to them, Be fruitful and multiply and fill the earth.

Genesis 9:1 MEV The sons of Noah who went forth from the ark were Shem, Ham, and Japheth. Ham was the father of Canaan. These were the three sons of Noah, and from them the whole earth was populated. Genesis 9:18-19 MEV

The entire account of Noah and the ark is yet another type, shadow, similitude, and pattern of God's plan for the redemption of mankind, but; we will just look at one aspect of the greater prophetic pattern encompassing Noah and his three sons.

Each one of us is a descendant of one of Noah's three sons, and the Lord God Almighty has an awesome plan for each our lives (Jeremiah 29:11). Father God appointed and determined the exact time and place you and I would enter and exit this earthly experience we call life. Our Abba, Father is truly awesome and worthy of our praise!

You take account of my wandering; put my tears in Your bottle; are they not in Your book? Psalm 56:8 MEV

Your eyes saw me unformed, yet in Your book all my days were written, before any of them came into being. Psalm 139:16 MEV

And He made from one [common origin, one source, one blood] all nations of men to settle on the face of the earth, having definitely determined [their] allotted periods of time and the fixed boundaries of their habitations (their settlements, lands, and abodes), so that they should seek God, in the hope that they might find Him, although He is not far from each one of us. Acts 17:26-27 AMPC

Therefore, our heavenly Father God has specifically and purposely chosen who would be alive right now to prepare the world for the single most important event ever to come to pass, which is the return of the King of kings and Lord of lords, King Jesus; to rule and reign forever! Wow, just contemplate that incredible Truth for a while.

For this portion of our study, we have chosen to begin post flood after these eight people exited the ark, the new beginning for mankind on earth. The number eight is the number of new beginnings in Scripture.

For if God did not spare the angels that sinned, but cast them down to hell and delivered them into chains of darkness to be kept for judgment; and if He did not spare the ancient world, but saved Noah, a preacher of righteousness, with seven others, when He brought a flood upon the world of the ungodly; II Peter 2:4-5 MEV

We know from the Scriptures that these eight people, and only eight; were Noah and his wife, and their three sons and their wives.

The sons of Noah who went forth from the ark were Shem, Ham, and Japheth. Ham was the father of Canaan. These were the three sons of Noah, and from them the whole earth was populated. Genesis 9:18-19 MEV

We can see revealed that every tribe and people group on our planet came from these three sons of Noah, as outlined in the table of the seventy nations of the earth in Genesis 10. We know from Scripture that (Genesis 10:21) that Japheth was the first born, and Shem the second, and Ham the third born. (Genesis 9:24) We only point this out so you can make note of the fact that God doesn't get troubled by birth order to establish importance, honor, inheritance, blessing, or whatever.

This is a custom or tradition established by man, not by God. The Word of God was spoken and written by the prophets selected by God; as each of them were inspired to speak, write, or act by the Holy Spirit. (Genesis 18:17, Genesis 20:7, II Samuel 23:2, Amos 3:7, Acts 3:18-21, II Timothy 3:16, II Peter 1:21, Revelation 10:7) The point is that the Holy Spirit is

The Author of the Bible, therefore; Holy Spirit chose to list these sons of Noah in this order: Shem, Ham, and Japheth, meaning that Shem was honored and blessed above his brothers by Father God.

From these three sons, the earth was repopulated. It has been written by Jewish sages that in the Hebrew language Shem means "dusky" and Ham means "black" and Japheth means "fair." We are not reporting this as absolute fact, just sharing what has traditionally been handed down through the writings of past generations of the ancient Hebrew people and scholars of the Hebrew language.

We do know through the comprehensive research of other trained intellectuals, and through the advancement of DNA scientific testing, where the seventy (70) nations recorded in Genesis chapter ten spread out and settled over time. Science ultimately proves the bible is true, not the other way around. In the beginning, the seven continents and the various cultures were all one land mass before God divided the continents, people groups, and languages in Peleg's generation, as we see recorded in the Scriptures.

To Eber were born two sons. The name of one was Peleg, for in his days the earth was divided; his brother's name was Joktan. Genesis 10:25 MEV

Two sons were born to Eber: The name of one was Peleg, for in his days the earth was divided, and the name of his brother was Joktan. I Chronicles 1:19 MEV

The name Peleg literally means "Division" and the name Joktan literally means "Smaller" and there is much revelation to be gleaned from the inspired names of people and places throughout the Scriptures.

It has been well established in the written Word (Genesis 1:26, Isaiah 61:1, Luke 3:22, I John 5:7) that we humans were created in the image of the Creator, which we express as the Godhead, or the Holy Trinity, which is the Father, Son, and Holy Spirit, and the three are one.

We humans are three-part triune beings also, just like our Father.

May the very God of peace sanctify you completely. And I pray to God that your whole spirit, soul, and body be preserved blameless unto the coming of our Lord Jesus Christ. I Thessalonians 5:23 MEV

For the word of God is alive, and active, and sharper than any two-edged sword, piercing even to the division of soul and spirit, of joints and marrow, and able to judge the thoughts and intents of the heart. Hebrews 4:12 MEV

The Trinity Pattern

As we can see in the Scripture above, the soul and the spirit could not be divided if they were not two different entities. As the Bible so clearly teaches, we are spirit beings, and we have a soul, and we live in our body.

Shem constitutes our spiritual (spirit) man, Ham our physical (body) man, and Japheth our intellectual (soul) man. Our spirit man is the part of us that knows God after our spirits are born-again or born from above. (Proverbs 20:27, John 3:3-6, I Corinthians 2:10-14) and our soul (mind, will, and emotions) and our body (fleshly lusts and desires) must be renewed, controlled, and brought under submission by us.

Our soul & body does not become born-again. As our spirit man is fed the *Bread of Life*, which is the Word of God, and becomes stronger, and our worldly beliefs and mindsets become renewed and come in line with the Truth, then we can crucify our flesh and bring every thought captive to the obedience of Christ. (Romans 7:15-20, Romans 12:1-2, I Corinthians 6:20, Galatians 5:16-17, 24-26, Colossians 3:5-10, II Corinthians 10:5)

What we feed grows and what we starve dies. We shall discuss this process of body and soul submission resulting in sanctification and give patterns and examples of this Truth, in future teachings within other chapters in this volume.

Can there be any doubt that Shem represents our spiritual man? There are two basic forms of religion in the world today, and they are monotheism and polytheism. Monotheists worship one god and polytheists worship multiple gods. Abraham and his offspring are the originators of all the monotheistic religions of the world; Judaism, Christianity, and the Muslims, in which even our secular history books document and refer to as the Abrahamic religions, and Abram is the descendant of Shem. (Genesis 11:10-26)

Together our spirit, soul, and body constitute the whole person, just as Shem, Ham, and Japheth represents all of mankind over the whole earth.

God Almighty made a blood covenant with Abraham and said: *for I have made you the father of a multitude of nations.* Genesis 17:5b MEV and *in you all families of the earth will be blessed.* Genesis 12:3b MEV We know this is the Truth. Unequivocally first and foremost, Jesus Christ was the forty-second generation that came after father Abraham (Matthew 1:1, Luke 3:34) and all the people of the earth have been blessed through Jesus, but; secondly (per ancient Jewish tradition and recorded history); through Abraham's three wives:

Sarah, the mother of Isaac; is the daughter of Shem, (Genesis 12:17-20, Genesis 20:12) and Hagar, the mother of Ishmael; is the daughter of Ham, (Genesis 12:16, Genesis 16:1-3) and Keturah, the mother of six princes; (Genesis 25:1-2) is the daughter of Japheth, per some Jewish sages. The account of Abraham, Keturah, and their offspring are also found in the ancient Hebrew history books of Jasher and Jubilees along with the works of the first century Levite historian Josephus.

The Bible is not obviously clear who Keturah is, so; you can choose to believe what you wish about from whom Keturah is a descendant. We do know that the descendants of Japheth intermingled in the lands inhabited by the descendants of Shem because the Scriptures record that Japheth's offspring would dwell intermingled in the tents, or settlements of Shem.

When Noah awoke from his wine and knew what his younger son had done to him, he said, Canaan be cursed! He will be a servant of servants to his brothers. He also said, Blessed be the Lord God of Shem, and let Canaan be his servant. May God enlarge Japheth, and may he dwell in the tents of Shem, and may Canaan be his servant. Genesis 9:24-27 MEV

It is interesting to note that Noah said that Shem would be blessed by God, and that God would enlarge Japheth, but Canaan would be their servant.

Sarah was Abrahams half-sister because they had the same father, (Genesis 20:12) therefore a descendant of Shem; and she was blessed by God because her son Isaac was the son of the covenant promise. Hagar was Sarah's maidservant from Egypt, and a descendant of Canaan, who was Ham's son; and God enlarged Japheth and they did scatter-out and dwell among the Semitic people.

Fast forward through time several hundred years and forty-two generations to early first century AD, to the life and ministry of our Lord Jesus Christ; and we shall find that this God ordained, and established order of Shem, Ham, and Japheth continues.

The entire world came seeking to serve and worship Jesus, the promised Messiah and King. (Isaiah 7:14, Isaiah 9:6-7, Micah 5:2, Revelation 5:1-10)

I saw in the night visions, and there was one like the Son of Man coming with the clouds of heaven. He came to the Ancient of Days and was presented before Him. There was given to Him dominion, and glory, and a kingdom, that all peoples, nations, and languages should serve Him. His dominion is an everlasting dominion, which shall not pass away, and His kingdom that which shall not be destroyed. Daniel 7:13-14 MEV

The very night that Jesus was born, there were shepherds abiding in the fields surrounding Bethlehem, keeping watch over their herds, when an angel of the Lord came to tell them of the good news: For unto you is born this day in the City of David a Savior, who is Christ the Lord. Luke 2:11 MEV The shepherds went in haste to seek and find the Christ child. These shepherds were the descendants of Shem, the very first people to seek and worship (Luke 2:20) the newborn King Jesus.

Not long after the birth of Jesus, there came wise men, or Magi; from the east to worship the newborn King of the Jews, and to present Him with gifts. (Matthew 2:11) These wise men from the east (Daniel 2:48), had been taught by the men Daniel had trained in the land of Shinar, or Babylon (Genesis 10:10) about the prophesied King (gift of gold) and great High Priest (gift of frankincense) that was to die (gift of myrrh) as the Savior of the world. These Magi from the east were the second people to seek and worship Jesus. These men are descendants of Ham.

Now at Jerusalem, a few days before the real feast of Passover, another prophetic type and shadow of things to come; we see recorded another prophetic declaration: So the Pharisees said among themselves, See, you are gaining nothing! Look, the world has followed Him! John 12:19 MEV They were of course speaking prophetically of Jesus Christ.

Now there were some Greeks among those who went up to worship at the feast. They came to Philip, who was from Bethsaida of Galilee, and asked Him, Sir, we want to see Jesus. John 12:20-21 MEV

These Greek Gentiles came to behold Jesus and to worship Him, not just come to get something from Him. These Greeks, which are descendants of Javan; (and Javan is the Hebrew word for Greek) the progenitor of the Greeks (Genesis 10:2, Daniel 8:21, Zechariah 9:13), were the last third of the world to seek and worship Jesus. These men are descendants of Japheth.

Now, the entire world, represented by the sons of Shem, Ham, and Japheth; had come to seek and worship Jesus, and Jesus knew this because He responded to His disciples by saying: The hour is come, for the Son of Man to be glorified. John 12:23 MEV. Meaning, of course; that the divinely pre-set time period of His passion had come.

The passion of Christ was, is, and always will be to redeem all mankind from eternal separation from the Father, so the Father could give mankind to the Son as His bride. (Psalm 2:8, John 3:35, John 6:40, John 17:2, Acts 2:21, Romans 10:13, Ephesians 5:2, Revelation 19:7-8)

Jesus also said: And if I be lifted up from the earth, I will draw all men to Myself. He said this to signify by what kind of death He would die. John 12:32-33 MEV

The whole world participated in the crucifixion and death of Jesus.

First, the chief priests, elders, scribes (which constitute the Great Sanhedrin) and the Jews took the moral and legal responsibility of Jesus' crucifixion: When Pilate saw that he could not prevail, but rather that unrest was beginning, he took water and washed his hands before the crowd, saying, I am innocent of the blood of this righteous Man. See to it yourselves. Then all the people answered, His blood be on us and on our children! Matthew 27:24-25 MEV (also see Mark 15:1, John 19:6-16, Acts 5:27-28) These are the sons of Shem.

A man named Simon, from Cyrene: They compelled a man named Simon from Cyrene, the father of Alexander and Rufus, as he was passing through from the country, to bear Jesus' cross. Mark 15:21 MEV (also see Luke 23:26). This Libyan physically assisted in the death of Jesus on the cross. Simon, which means *hears and obeys;* of Cyrene was a descendant of Ham.

The Roman soldiers led Jesus to the place of the Skull (which is Calvary in Latin), physically executed the crucifixion and witnessed His death. (see Luke 23:33-47, John 19:32-34) These Italians are descendants of Japheth.

The entire world sought to hear the Gospel preached.

On the birth-day of the church age, the day of Pentecost; Peter stood and preached the very first Gospel message to the: Men of Judea, and all you that dwell in Jerusalem.... Acts 2:14b MEV (also see Acts 2:22, Acts 2:36) These men of Judea are descendants of Shem.

Not long after this Philip the Evangelist (Acts 21:8) was sent by an angel of the Lord (Acts 8:26) to the desert road that runs between Jerusalem and Gaza. Once there Philip saw a man in a chariot reading the Scriptures, and the Holy Spirit then directed Philip to join this very wealthy and educated Ethiopian man

The Trinity Pattern

that had come to worship and was traveling by chariot back to his home in Ethiopia (Acts 8:27-29). Philip joined this man and preached unto him Jesus. (Acts 8:35) This east African man is a son of Ham.

Approximately ten years after Jesus' passion, Peter was sent by an angel to the house of Cornelius, a centurion of the band called the Italian band (Acts 10:1) to preach the Gospel. These were the first Gentiles (Acts 10:28) to receive the Word of God (Acts 11:1). All these people from the house of Cornelius are the descendants of Japheth.

The three Synoptic Gospels were written by, and for; the whole world.

The Gospel of Matthew was written by Matthew, as he was inspired by the Holy Ghost. Levi (see Matthew 9:9, Mark 2:14, Luke 5:27) better known to us as Matthew, is a Jewish man and a descendant of Shem.

The Gospel of Mark was written by John Mark, as he was directed by his spiritual father (I Peter 5:13) and inspired by the Holy Spirit. Barnabas was his mother's relative. (Acts 4:36, Colossians 4:10) Early Church records state that John Mark was born in Cyrene, Libya; and that Mark's father was Libyan and died when Mark was a young man, and he and his Jewish mother relocated to Jerusalem after his father's death. This would make Mark a descendant of Ham.

The Gospel of Luke was written by Luke the Greek physician (Colossians 4:14) believed to be from Antioch, as he was inspired by the Holy Ghost. Doctor Luke, the Greek physician; is a descendant of Japheth.

Of course, the will of God has not and shall not ever change. (Malachi 3:6) Our heavenly Father desires that every person come to the saving knowledge of His Son, Jesus Christ; the Savior of the world, (I Timothy 2:1-6) and to repent of your sins and invite Him to become the Lord and Savior of your life, because Jesus is the only way to life eternal with Him in our heavenly home.

Jesus said unto him, I AM the way, the truth, and the life. No one comes to the Father, except through Me. John 14:6 MEV And Jesus said: For the Son of Man has come to seek and to save that which was lost. Luke 19:10 MEV

Then Peter, filled with the Holy Spirit, said to them, Rulers of the people and elders of Israel: If we today are being examined concerning a good deed done to a crippled man, how this man has been healed, be it known to you all, and to all the people of Israel, that by the name of Jesus Christ of Nazareth, whom you crucified, whom God raised from the dead, by Him this man stands before you whole. He is the stone you builders rejected, which has become the cornerstone. There is no salvation in any other, for there is no other name under heaven given among men by which we must be saved. Acts 4:8-12 MEV

Is not our Lord and Savior amazing! More reasons to be in awe of Him and His Word. This study illustrates one of the many patterns within the Scriptures how God proves repeatedly that His Word is Truth and our faith is in Him alone. (Psalm 33:4, Psalm 119:160, John 17:17, II Timothy 2:15)

Remember the former things of old, for I am God, and there is no other; I am God, and there is no one like Me, declaring the end from the beginning, and from ancient times the things that are not yet done, saying, My counsel shall stand, and I will do all My good pleasure, Isaiah 46:9-10 MEV

We all are now one new man through our common union in Christ, through Christ, and because of Jesus Christ. All mankind, represented by Shem, Ham, and Japheth; now equals the Jew and the Gentiles; (Ephesians 2:14-15) which all took part in the crucifixion of the Lord of glory, therefore; every individual that has repented of their dead works (Acts 2:36-39,

Acts 4:10-12) and accepted Jesus as their personal Savior and Lord are commanded to partake of the Lord's Supper in remembrance of the finished work of the cross and the ransom that Jesus has paid-in-full for us all through His broken, bruised, and pierced body and His precious and ever powerful shed blood.

Surely he has borne our grief and carried our sorrows; yet we esteemed him stricken, smitten of God, and afflicted. But he was wounded for our transgressions, he was bruised for our iniquities; the chastisement of our peace was upon him, and by his stripes we are healed. All of us like sheep have gone astray; each of us has turned to his own way, but the Lord has laid on him the iniquity of us all. Isaiah 53:4-6 MEV

And He [that same Jesus Himself] is the propitiation (the atoning sacrifice) for our sins, and not for ours alone but also for [the sins of] the whole world. I John 2:2 AMPC

I have received of the Lord that which I delivered to you: that the Lord Jesus, on the night in which He was betrayed, took bread. When He had given thanks, He broke it and said, Take and eat. This is My body which is broken for you. Do this in remembrance of Me. In the same manner He took the cup after He had supper, saying, This cup is the new covenant in

My blood. Do this, as often as you drink it, in remembrance of Me. As often as you eat this bread and drink this cup, you proclaim the Lord's death until He comes. I Corinthians 11:23-26 MEV

All of mankind participated in the torture and death of Jesus so that all of mankind that turn from their sinful past and professes Jesus as their Lord and Savior can share in the Lord's Supper together, in remembrance of our King's sacrifice for us all. Amen.

In review, the Godhead; Father, Son, and Holy Spirit are three yet one. We human beings, made in the image and likeness of our heavenly Father are three-part beings; spirit (conscience, communion, wisdom), soul (mind, will, emotions), and body (flesh, blood, bone). And we see clearly in Scripture; and through types, shadows, similitudes, and patterns, we are three-part triune beings. We must receive revelation of this foundational Truth to be able to fully comprehend why we are here, which is to continue the work that Jesus started as our example.

This is the Believer's Mandate.

Chapter Five

The Master's key

Foundational Truth: Jesus taught with parables, patterns, and similitudes, and Jesus taught the Parable of the Sower is the key to the revelatory comprehension all the parables.

For I am the Lord, I do not change; therefore you, O sons of Jacob, are not consumed. Malachi 3:16 MEV

From before You have laid the foundation of the earth, and the heavens are the work of Your hands. They shall perish, but You shall endure; indeed, all of them shall wear out like a garment; like a robe You shall change them, and they shall pass away, but You are the same, and Your years shall have no end. Psalm 102:25-27 MEV

Jesus Christ is the same yesterday, and today, and forever. Hebrews 13:8 MEV

I have also spoken to [you by] the prophets, and I have multiplied visions [for you] and [have appealed to you] through parables acted out by the prophets. Hosea 12:10 AMPC

And the word of the Lord came to me, saying, Son of man, put forth a riddle and speak a parable or allegory to the house of Israel; Ezekiel 17:1-2 AMPC

And utter a parable against the rebellious house [of Judah] and say to them, Thus says the Lord God: put on a pot; put it on and also pour water into it. Ezekiel 24:3 AMPC

Give ear, O my people, to my teaching; incline your ears to the word of my mouth. I will open my mouth in a parable (in instruction by numerous examples); I will utter dark sayings of old [that hide important truth] which we have heard and known, and our fathers have told us. Psalm 78:1-3 AMPC

Father God never changes, and the Word of God never changes, and Jesus never changes. I deeply appreciate these Truths because we can, without any reservation; build our lives on the Rock of Ages, which is the everlasting Word of God.

Trust in the Lord forever, for in God the Lord we have an everlasting rock. Isaiah 26:4 MEV

Jesus taught with parables and we count a total of forty-six parables within the four gospels, counting the teaching in the Gospel of John chapter 10:1-18 about the sheep, the gate, and the Shepherd as one parable. Of course, several of these parables are in one or more of the Gospels, and if you counted all of them within the four, we come up with a total of more than sixty parable accounts, and each one of them are very important, and we must study them all, however; we are going to focus on one of the many, because Jesus said if you do not understand this parable, then we will not understand any of the parables.

One might say that the Parable of the Sower is the "Master's key" to unlocking the mysteries that the Lord wants to reveal to us through His use of parables and similitudes. There have been many good, solid teachings about the Parable of the Sower through the past generations, therefore; some of you that are faithful to study your Bible will be tempted to zone-out a bit here because you believe you have revelation of the Parable of the Sower, however; we would like to encourage you to stay focused with us, on the chance that you might see some detail revealed you have not seen before.

The Master's Key

The Parable of the Sower can be found in Matthew 13:3-23, Mark 4:1-20, and Luke 8:4-15, and we certainly need to study each one, however; we are going to use Mark's Gospel account as our primary Scripture reference.

Again Jesus began to teach beside the lake. And a very great crowd gathered about Him, so that He got into a ship in order to sit in it on the sea, and the whole crowd was at the lakeside on the shore. And He taught them many things in parables (illustrations or comparisons put beside truths to explain them), and in His teaching He said to them: Give attention to this! Behold, a sower went out to sow. And as he was sowing, some seed fell along the path, and the birds came and ate it up. Other seed [of the same kind] fell on ground full of rocks, where it had not much soil; and at once it sprang up, because it had no depth of soil; And when the sun came up, it was scorched, and because it had not taken root, it withered away. Other seed [of the same kind] fell among thorn plants, and the thistles grew and pressed together and utterly choked and suffocated it, and it yielded no grain. And other seed [of the same kind] fell into good soil (well adapted) soil and brought forth grain, growing up and increasing, and yielded up to thirty times as much, and sixty times as much, and even a hundred times as much as has been sown. And He said, He who has ears to hear. Let him be hearing [and let him consider, and comprehend]. Mark 4:1-9 AMPC

Obviously, Jesus was teaching before a very large gathering of people when he spoke out this parable. Jesus also ended His public teaching with a familiar, but sober closing. (It is recorded seven times in the synoptic gospels and seven times in the book of Revelation.) Jesus is admonishing the crowd to very carefully consider, ponder, and apply what they had just heard, because there is a deeper spiritual revelation behind the parable teachings that they must seek out the understanding. Everything Jesus said is important and life changing, however; anything He commanded us to do more than a dozen times should be a priority for us to comprehend and apply to our lives.

And as soon as He was alone, those who were around Him, with the Twelve [apostles], began to ask Him about the parables. And He said to them, To you has been entrusted the mystery of the kingdom of God [that is, the secret counsels of God which are hidden from the ungodly]; but for those outside [of our circle] everything becomes a parable, In order that they may [indeed] look and look but not see and perceive, and may hear and hear but not grasp and comprehend, lest haply they should turn again, and it [their willful rejection of the truth] should be forgiven them. Mark 4:10-12 AMPC

When Jesus began His public ministry: From that time Jesus began to preach, crying out, Repent (change your mind for the better, heartily amend your ways, with abhorrence of your past sins), for the kingdom of heaven is at hand. Matthew 4:17 AMPC

And He went about all Galilee, teaching in their synagogues and preaching the good news (Gospel) of the kingdom, and healing every disease and every weakness and infirmity among the people. Matthew 4:23 AMPC

Jesus was preaching and teaching the Truth to the people in very clear terms and examples as He was calling them to repent and to change their hearts, minds, and behaviors. As you read The Sermon on the Mount (Matthew 5-7) which is the first, longest and probably the most famous of all of Jesus' sermons, you can see that He was teaching in a very straightforward way.

Yes, He used types, shadows, and similitudes in this teaching, but; He also explained them as He progressed. As time went on though, Jesus' teaching was met with great resistance, hardheartedness, unbelief, scoffers, and religious pride and arrogance to the point that Jesus modified His methodology, and He was certain of the receptiveness of His audience before He shared the secrets of the kingdom with the hearers. Jesus first ascertained if His hearers were of a humble, teachable heart and mind before He shared His precious pearls, thus giving us all a living example of His words, teaching us: Do not give that which is holy (the sacred things) to the dogs, and do not throw your pearls before hogs, lest they trample upon them with their feet and turn and tear you in pieces. Matthew 7:6 AMPC

So, as Jesus' public ministry advanced, He began to increasingly use parables in His public teaching, and as is the case in the Parable of the Sower, He would then explain the deeper spiritual and seemingly veiled meaning of the parables to those individuals that were truly seeking the Truth with a humble heart. These are those that truly have "ears to hear" what the Master is teaching us.

Our heavenly Father doesn't hide things from us, He hides them for us to discover as we diligently seek Him. Jesus desires to reveal His kingdom secrets to

His true disciples that are spiritually hungry and are honest hearted believers that are truly committed to follow Jesus and are seeking His kingdom ways. Are you one of them? Good, let us hear and obey Jesus.

And He said to them, Do you not discern and understand this parable? How then is it possible for you to discern and understand all the parables? Mark 4:13 AMPC

Obviously, we understand that Jesus is not the guest speaker at some best practices seminar on proper seed bed selection at the annual farmer's convention, and He is not really lecturing on agriculture at all, but then again; it is also clear that many in the crowd did not understand His illustrative teachings, and still don't.

The New Testament was first written in the Greek language and here in this verse there were two Greek words that have been translated either "know" or "understand" in at least thirty of our most widely read English translations from original manuscripts of Scripture.

The first word translated "know/understand" here is the Greek word *Eido* which means to behold, perceive, grasp, or mentally see, comprehend and acknowledge a truth, and the second use of the word "know/

understand" is translated from the Greek word *Ginosko* which means to have intimate, applied knowledge or to experientially to know something. So, to paraphrase this verse and apply the expanded meaning of the Greek words *Eido* and *Ginosko* (as written in the original transcript of the Scriptures) helps us to gain revelation of what Jesus is teaching here.

So, another way this verse could be accurately spoken in our modern-day vernacular is (authors paraphrase): Hey, are you really paying attention? You guys have got to get this one. If you don't grasp and comprehend the spiritual truth illustrated by this comparison of things that you witness in the natural world in which you live, how then do you think you will be able to truly understand, apply, and experience the spiritual increase from any of these simple examples that I have spoken to you?

The sower sows the Word. The ones along the path are those who have the Word sown [in their hearts], but when they hear, Satan comes at once and [by force] takes away the message which is sown in them. And in the same way the ones sown upon stony ground are those who, when they hear the Word, at once receive and accept and welcome it with joy; and they have no real root in themselves, and so they endure for a little while; then when trouble or persecution arises on account of the Word, they immediately are offended (become displeased, indignant, resentful) and they stumble and fall away. And the ones sown among the thorns are others who hear the Word; then the cares and anxieties of the world and distractions of the age, and the pleasure and delight and false glamour and deceitfulness of riches, and the craving and passionate desire for other things creep in and choke and suffocate the Word, and it becomes fruitless. Mark 4:14-19 AMPC

Jesus is clearly teaching us that God's Word is the seed, and these first three soil types are examples of different heart conditions that exist among people. We know that the seed is flawless and perfect, so; the only variable that is possible here is the quality and condition of the soil that the seed falls upon.

The first soil type is the well-traveled, hard, compacted path and the seed never has a chance to sprout because it just lies on the hard surface and the enemy comes and *steals* the seed.

The second soil type is the thin soiled stony ground that the seed lands upon and just begins to sprout roots, but; because of the shallowness of the root system, as soon as the sun comes up and the young plant gets hot and distressed, the weak shallow-rooted young sprout is *killed*.

The third soil type is the thorny ground that the seed falls among and tries to take root and grow, but; the demands of the weeds and thorns that our small plant is competing with for nutrients, is thus choked-out and *destroyed* before it could get deeply rooted and established.

Jesus warns us very clearly about our enemy when He said: The thief does not come, except to steal and kill and destroy. I came that they may have life, and that they have it more abundantly. John 10:10 MEV The thief, the enemy of your soul; comes to steal the Word, kill the Word, and destroy the Word, consequently; stealing, killing, and destroying your real life source, the living Word.

We all can probably identify with these three individuals or "soil types" with some thought. The hard, well-traveled path is the hard-hearted type of person that might hear the Word, but; they don't give it any consideration or place in their life. The path people just keep living however they wish and they never really have any perceivable change in their lives or behavior.

The stony ground person is the one that might come to a church meeting or gathering where they hear the

Word and seem to believe and receive the Word, but; as soon as any trouble, hardship, or pressure comes their way, they are grumbling, complaining and basically allowing the situations of life (that come to all of us) to control them and kill their faith, joy, and peace. It seems the stony ground folks are forever the victim and often taking offense in many situations.

The thorny ground person is the church attender that claims to love the Lord and attends meetings when it doesn't conflict with their other scheduled events. They are always very busy. You know the type, they just don't have time to read their Bible, or pray, or volunteer, or anything else, because they are busy, busy, busy. However; they say things like "I had to work last Sunday, so; I couldn't come to church, but; the Lord knows my heart", or "I don't need to attend that bible study because I know the Bible already, and besides my daughter has dance class on that night." The thorny ground individual has many idols in their life, but; they have a very difficult time seeing this truth because of their love and devotion to their worldly priorities, pleasures, and pursuits.

Before we move forward to the next soil types, let's make sure we are abundantly clear here. The first three of the seven soil types are spiritually poor and unproductive lives that need some improvement and/or changes of priorities before the good Seed can take root, grow, and bear good fruit.

And those sown on good (well-adapted) soil are the ones who hear the Word and receive and accept and welcome it and bear fruit – some thirty times as much as was sown, some sixty times as much, and some [even] a hundred times as much. Mark 4:20 AMPC

Now we are sowing good seed in good soil. The good soil has had some preparation and attention, and it has been broken-up and prepared to receive the good Seed. The good ground is the person that has invited and accepted Jesus to be both their Savior and Lord of their lives. The good ground is a "born-again" spirit that has accepted the good Seed, which is the Word sown into their good, soft, and well-watered soil.

You have been regenerated (born again), not from a mortal origin (seed, sperm), but from one that is immortal by the ever living and lasting Word of God. For all flesh (mankind) is like grass, and all its glory (honor) like [the] flower of grass. The grass withers and the flower drops off, but the Word of the Lord (divine instruction, the Gospel) endures forever. And this Word is the good news which was preached to you. I Peter 1:23-25 AMPC

Once we make the decision to repent of our sins and believe on the Lord, and we ask Jesus to forgive us and thus become our Savior of our past and present, and the Lord of our future; this is just the beginning, not the destination. Becoming good soil is not something we can do on our own. We must yield to the work of the Holy Spirit and accept the gift of salvation through faith in the sacrifice Jesus made on the cross for all of mankind. *For by grace you have been saved through faith, and this is not of yourselves. It is the gift of God.* Ephesians 2:8 MEV

So, once we have been converted (born-again) into good soil, then what? How does that good soil become 30-fold soil, and 60-fold soil, and even 100-fold, fruit bearing soil?

The fourth soil type, or the good soil; is the born-again human spirit, or a baby Christian, and the fifth, sixth, and seventh good soil types are levels of spiritual growth and maturity. As we mature spiritually we bear more and greater spiritual fruit. Remember, this is the only thing we can take with us to heaven.

This is where many Christians get stagnant. They do not grow and mature for many reasons, however; we believe the main reason is the lack of good, sound teaching and discipleship training in the Church and thus we allow worldly distractions to define us and our priorities.

It is time for the body of believers to grow-up and become 30-fold, 60-fold, and even 100-fold fruitful followers of Jesus Christ. Amen. So, how do we realize this kind of growth?

The first step to understanding spiritual growth and becoming more skillful righteousness gardeners is to realize that we must become increasingly more and more like Jesus, and that is exactly what every born-again "good soil" believer is ultimately called to do. Each child of God is commanded, and therefore expected to fully submit to the process of being continuously transformed into the likeness of Jesus Christ. Folks, this is the Believer's Mandate.

Do you believe this? Let's make sure that we firmly establish this precept with the Truth.

And all of us, as with unveiled face, [because we] continue to behold [in the Word of God] as in a mirror the glory of the Lord, are constantly being transfigured into His very own image in ever increasing splendor and from one degree of glory to another; [for this comes] from the Lord [Who is] the Spirit. II Corinthians 3:18 AMPC

I appeal to you therefore, brethren, and beg of you in view of [all] the mercies of God, to make a decisive dedication of your bodies [presenting all your members and faculties] as living sacrifice, holy (devoted, consecrated) and well pleasing to God, which is your reasonable (rational, intelligent) service and spiritual worship. Do not be conformed to this world (this age), [fashioned after and adapted to its external, superficial customs], but be transformed (changed) by the [entire] renewal of your mind [by its new ideals and its new attitude], so that you may prove [for yourselves] what is the good and acceptable and perfect will of God, even the thing which is good and acceptable and perfect [in His sight for you]. Romans 12:1-2 AMPC

These words "transfigured" and "transformed" used in these two passages of Scripture above are the Greek word *Metamorphoo*, which is the root of the English word metamorphosis. We all can probably remember enough of our natural science class to know that this is exactly what a caterpillar experiences as he is being transformed in to a butterfly.

What the caterpillar would call doomsday, we call a beautiful butterfly. Selah

We can plainly see here that Paul is writing to the Church and telling them and us, that as born-again believer's and disciples of Jesus, each one of us must deal with our bodies and our souls. This is the will of the Father for all true followers of Jesus Christ.

This progressive development of being transfigured and transformed into the image and likeness of Jesus is what we commonly refer to as sanctification. Holiness and sanctification are not popular teaching topics in many of our churches today, and that is unfortunate because this is what all believers are called to and it truly is a beautiful thing, so; let's make sure we know and fully comprehend what sanctification is, and how to be doers of the word, not just hearers.

Sanctification: To be set apart; separated for a particular use, service, or work. To be made holy, consecrated, or sacred. The state of proper functioning.

To sanctify someone or something is to set that person or thing apart for the plans and purposes intended by its Master and Creator.

If there is any shred of doubt remaining in your mind, here are some additional Words from the Lord God Almighty about His desire for you and me to be sanctified. Folks, we are not supposed to look or act like the world.

For I am the Lord who brings you up out of the land of Egypt to be your God. Therefore you shall be holy, for I am holy. Leviticus 11:45 MEV

And the Lord spoke to Moses, saying: Speak to all the congregation of the children of Israel, and say to them: You shall be holy, for I the Lord your God am holy. Leviticus 19:1-2 MEV

Consecrate yourselves therefore, and be holy, for I am the Lord your God. You shall keep My statutes, and do them; I am the Lord who sanctifies you. Leviticus 20:7-8 MEV

You shall be holy unto Me; for I the Lord am holy and have separated you from other peoples, that you should be Mine. Leviticus 20:26 MEV

Therefore you shall keep My commandments and do them: I am the Lord. You shall not defile My holy name, but I will be sanctified among the children of Israel: I am the Lord who sanctifies you, who brought you out of the land of Egypt, to be your God: I am the Lord. Leviticus 22:31-33 MEV

Here are some New Testament Scriptures that are witnessing to these Old Testament Scriptures that command us to live holy, consecrated, separated, sanctified lives, separated out from the ways of the secular world.

So brace up your minds; be sober (circumspect, morally alert): set your hope wholly and unchangeably on the grace (divine favor) that is coming to you when Jesus Christ (the Messiah) is revealed. [Live] as children of obedience [to God]; do not conform yourselves to the evil desires [that governed you] in your former ignorance [when you did not know the requirements of the Gospel]. But as the One Who called you is holy, you yourselves also be holy in all your conduct and manner of living. For it is written, You shall be holy, for I am holy. I Peter 1:13-16 AMPC

Furthermore, brethren, we beg and admonish you in [virtue of our union with] the Lord Jesus, that [you follow the instructions which] you learned from us about how you ought to walk so as to please and gratify God, as indeed you are doing, [and] that you do so even more and more abundantly [attaining yet greater perfection in living this life]. For you know what charges and precepts we gave you [on the authority and by the inspiration of] the Lord Jesus. For this is the will of God, that you should be consecrated (separated and set apart for pure and holy living): that you should abstain and shrink from all sexual vice, that each one of you should know how to possess (control, manage) his own body in consecration (purity, separated from things profane) and honor, not [to be used] in the passion of lust like the heathen, who are ignorant of the true God and have no knowledge of His will, that no man transgress and overreach his brother and defraud him in this matter or defraud his brother in business. For the Lord is an avenger in all these things, as we have already warned you solemnly and told you plainly. For God has not called us to impurity but to consecration [to dedicate ourselves to the most thorough purity]. Therefore whoever disregards (sets aside and rejects this) disregards not man but God, Whose [very] Spirit [Whom] He gives to you is holy (chaste, pure). I Thessalonians 4:1-8 AMPC

We hope at this point you are beginning to get revelation that although your spirit man is born-again, however; your other two parts of your three-part triune being, (your body and your soul) are not born-again and we are commanded by God Almighty to deal with our bodies and our souls. Here are additional Scriptures that continue to build on this foundational Truth that we are charged to grow and mature spiritually, thus we must learn to control our bodies, renew our minds, and separate ourselves from the world and all its carnal ungodliness. This means that you and I must make the quality choice every day to follow in Jesus' footsteps and live Holy Spirit-led lives.

For the grace of God (His unmerited favor and blessing) has come forward (appeared) for the deliverance from sin and the eternal salvation for all mankind. It has trained us to reject and renounce all ungodliness (irreligion) and worldly (passionate) desires, to live discreet (temperate, self-controlled), upright, devout (spiritually whole) lives in this present world, awaiting and looking for the [fulfillment, the realization of our] blessed hope, even the glorious appearing of our great God and Savior Christ Jesus (the Messiah, the Anointed One), Who gave Himself on our behalf that He might redeem us (purchase our freedom) from all iniquity and purify for Himself a people [to be peculiarly His own, a people who are] eager and enthusiastic about [living a life that is good and filled with] beneficial deeds. Titus 2:11-14 AMPC

Do not be unequally yoked with unbelievers [do not make mismated alliances with them or come under a different yoke with them, inconsistent with your faith]. For what partnership have right living and right standing with God with iniquity and lawlessness? Or how can light have fellowship with darkness? What harmony can there be between Christ and Belial [the devil]? Or what has a believer in common with an unbeliever? What agreement [can there be between] a temple of God and idols? For we are the temple of the living God; even as God said, I will dwell in and with and among them and will walk in and with and among them, and I will be their God, and they shall be My people." So, come out from among [unbelievers], and separate (sever) yourselves from them, says the Lord, and touch not [any] unclean thing; then I will receive you kindly and treat you with favor, and I will be a Father to you, and you shall be My sons and daughters, says the Lord Almighty. Therefore, since these [great] promises are ours, beloved, let us cleanse ourselves from everything that contaminates and defiles body and spirit, and bring [our] consecration to completeness in the [reverential] fear of God. II Corinthians 6:14-7:1 AMPC

Apostle Paul is writing to the Church in Corinth, and of course to you and me; and Paul is quoting from and referencing the following Old Testament Scriptures in this passage to the Church: Exodus 29:45, Leviticus 26:12, Jeremiah 32:38, Ezekiel 37:27, Isaiah 52:11, Ezekiel 20:34, 41 and II Samuel 7:14.

These numerous Old Testament Scriptures contain the "great promises" that Paul is referring to in this passage, that are ours, if we are obedient to the Word and walk in the reverential fear of the Lord, separated from the world system and its ways.

These are not the only promises that are ours, because the Bible is full of Father God's promises to His family. It has been estimated that the Bible contains more than seven thousand promises, and they are all available to those that love Jesus and follow Him.

Is this not a clear instruction for our sanctification? Again, we are called to become increasingly more and more like Jesus in our daily walk with Him. Paul also wrote to the Church in Ephesus, and Corinth, and Philippi, and Thessalonica, and to us, that we children are to become imitators of our Father God.

Therefore be imitators of God [copy Him and follow His example] as well-beloved children [imitate their Father]. Ephesians 5:1 AMPC

So I urge you and implore you, be imitators of me. I Corinthians 4:16 AMPC

Pattern yourselves after me [follow my example], as I imitate and follow Christ (the Messiah). I Corinthians 11:1 AMPC

Brethren, together follow my example and observe those who live after the pattern we have set for you. Philippians 3:17 AMPC

And you [set yourselves to] become imitators of us and [through us] of the Lord Himself, for you welcomed our message in [spite of] much persecution, with joy [inspired] by the Holy Spirit; so that you [thus] became a pattern to all believers (those who adhere to, trust in, and rely on Christ Jesus) in Macedonia and Achaia (most of Greece). I Thessalonians 1:6-7 AMPC

And the High Priestly prayer of our Lord Jesus Christ recorded in the Gospel of John further clarifies for us what God's will is for all His children.

Sanctify them [purify, consecrate, separate them for Yourself, make them holy] by the Truth; Your Word is Truth. Just as You sent Me into the world, I also have sent them into the world. John 17:17-18 AMPC

Then Jesus said to them again, Peace to you! [Just] as the Father has sent Me forth, so I am sending you. John 20:21 AMPC

And here are some additional direct oracles from our Lord Jesus as He was teaching and preaching throughout Israel regarding the precept of sanctification.

You, therefore, must be perfect, [growing into complete maturity of godliness in mind and character, having reached the proper height of virtue and integrity], as your heavenly Father is perfect. Matthew 5:48 AMPC

Jesus said to him, If you would be perfect, go and sell what you have, and give to the poor, and you will have treasure in heaven. And come, follow Me. Matthew 19:21 MEV

The English word "perfect" used in Matthew 5:48 and Matthew 19:21 is translated from the Greek word *Teleios.* We can gain a much greater understanding of exactly what our Lord Jesus is commanding of us by looking at the definition of the Greek word *Teleios,* which is: Having reached its end; complete, perfect, full grown, mature, lacking nothing, fully developed.

Epaphras greets you. He is one of you, a servant of Christ, always laboring fervently for you in prayers, that you may stand mature and complete in the entire will of God. Colossians 4:12 MEV The word "mature" is the Greek word *Teleios.*

Until we all come into the unity of the faith and the knowledge of the Son of God, into a complete man, to the measure of the stature of the fullness of Christ. Ephesians 4:13 MEV The word "complete" is the Greek word *Teleios.*

But let patience perfect its work, that you may be perfect and complete, lacking nothing. James 1:4 MEV The word "perfect" used twice here, is again the Greek word *Teleios.*

Our heavenly Father has asked His family to grow-up. We are all called to spiritually grow-up and become perfect like Him, just as Jesus came to show us the Father by imitation, we are then to imitate Jesus in every way. Do you believe Jesus would command us to do something we could not do?

So Jesus answered them by saying, I assure you, most solemnly I tell you, the Son is able to do nothing of Himself (of His own accord); but He is able to do only what He sees the Father doing, for whatever the Father does is what the Son does in the same way [in His turn]. John 5:19 AMPC

I am able to do nothing from Myself [independently, of My own accord – but only as I am taught by God and as I get His orders]. Even as I hear, I judge [I decide as I am bidden to decide. As the voice comes to Me, so I give a decision], and My judgment is right (just, righteous), because I do not seek or consult My own will [I have no desire to do what is pleasing to Myself, My own aim, My own purpose] but only the will and pleasure of the Father Who sent Me. John 5:30 AMPC

For I have come down from heaven not to do My own will and purpose but to do the will and purpose of Him Who sent Me. John 6:38 AMPC

So Jesus added, When you have lifted up the Son of Man [on the cross] you will realize (know, understand) that I am He [for Whom you look] and that I do nothing of Myself (of My own accord or on My own authority), but I say [exactly] what My Father has taught Me. John 8:28 AMPC

Jesus made it very clear that He could say or do nothing apart from the Father. Jesus came to show us the Father, and to do the Fathers will in complete, total, and absolute submission and obedience. Likewise, we are commanded to imitate Jesus in each and in every way. Therefore, we are to be growing, maturing, and completing the sanctification process as we yield to the work of the Holy Spirit, and living spiritually fruitful lives. This is Father God's will for all His children.

Jesus also made it very clear that separated from Him we can do nothing, so; here is the answer to how we accomplish and fulfill this command to become just like Jesus. We choose Him, and keep choosing Him daily, and consistently and faithfully walk in His ways.

I am the true vine, and My Father is the vinedresser. Every branch in Me that bears no fruit, He takes away. And every branch that bears fruit, He prunes, that it may bear more fruit. You are already clean through the word which I have spoken to you. Remain in Me, as I also remain in you. As the branch cannot bear fruit by itself, unless it remains in the vine, neither can you, unless you remain in Me. I am the vine, you are the branches. He who remains in Me, and I in him, bears much fruit. For without Me you can do nothing. If a man does not remain in Me, he is thrown out as a branch and withers. And they gather them and throw them into the fire, and they are burned. If you remain in Me, and My words remain in you, you will ask whatever you desire, and it shall be done for you. My Father is glorified by this, that you bear much fruit; so you will be My disciples. John 15:1-8 MEV

However, you and I must choose to submit to this process. Sanctification does not just happen. We must make the free-will choice abide in Christ. We must keep making this choice every day of our lives here on earth.

We all have been given a free will by Father God, and He will not force us to do anything against our free will, including acceptance of Jesus or the Holy Spirit. We must choose to surrender our will so we can do His will for our lives, just like Jesus did; and only then will we bear much fruit: thirty, sixty, or a hundred times as much. We are to bear much spiritual fruit because this brings glory to our heavenly Father.

The Believer's Mandate

Finally, brethren, farewell (rejoice)! Be strengthened (perfected, completed, made what you ought to be); be encouraged and consoled and comforted; be of the same [agreeable] mind one with another; live in peace, and [then] the God of love [Who is the Source of affection, goodwill, love, and benevolence toward men] and the Author and Promoter of peace will be with you. II Corinthians 13:11 AMPC

This is the Believer's Mandate.

CHAPTER SIX

God's will

Foundational Truth: God's written Word is God's will for all mankind.

This building block in our spiritual foundation is so incredibly vital to our lives that it is literally impossible to overstate its importance. We simply must gain a firm grasp and comprehension of this simple yet so profound statement. So many people I have encountered in my five decades of traveling, working, teaching, preaching, and just living, have not received revelation of this foundational Truth, and frankly; I used to be one of them.

I can personally testify to the fact that many professing Christians do not know that God's Word is His will because I have heard too many individuals that confess to know Jesus say something like this: "Wow,

I wish I knew God's will for me" or "Yeah, I been a hoping and a praying that I will hear from God about this situation in my life" Well, here's the deal folks, you nor I ever have to wonder what God's will is because He so graciously wrote it all down for us and it is called the *Holy Bible*, and if you don't know what God's will is for you; it's because you have chosen not to read it and seek it.

None of us have any legitimate excuses to be word starved, and I would like to touch upon this in some measure before we move forward. I shared in greater detail some of my life experiences and personal testimony in the introduction of this book, so; I won't elaborate now any further about my journey except to say that I have a deep appreciation for the awesome men and women of God that I have encountered during my own personal spiritual transformation and my continuing pursuit of spiritual growth and of my faith. I thank the Lord for each one of the dedicated and anointed servants of God that help us all grow in our walk with the Lord. So, even if you struggle to find a local church to attend, we all can still get real help with our faith life and spiritual development.

God's Word is more accessible today than ever before through many different media sources, so

God's Will

regardless of our school, work, and leisure schedules, we can access solid anointed teaching and preaching at any time of day or night as our schedule allows. So, combined with the fact that we all have one or more copies of the Bible in our homes, we can literally read, listen and/or watch anointed preaching and teaching twenty-four hours a day, seven days a week through Christian books, CD's, DVD's, cable television, satellite television, through the internet on our computers, and our smartphones. We simply do not have any excuses. No, the truth is many choose to prioritize other activities and place a greater value on other things to our relationship with Jesus Christ.

Now, in a humble attempt to imitate the greatest Teacher of all time, I would like to share a short parable with you to help us understand this profound Truth.

Let us imagine that you receive a phone call tomorrow from some big city Lawyer that is a partner in a world famous Legal firm, that everybody recognizes and has heard of. And this bona fide Attorney specializes in Estate Law and thus, he is the legal executor of the vast holdings of their now-deceased client's huge estate.

This Attorney is now calling to inform you that in-fact you are a named legal co-heir to this deceased relative's multi-billion-dollar fortune. You and a handful of others are the confirmed legal heirs of the entirety of this massive estate. Do you think that you would be willing to listen to what this Attorney would have to say?

Well, yes, I believe we all would take the time to listen. As the Attorney continues, he informs you that they had already confirmed that you are a legal co-heir, and that there are absolutely no encumbrances whatsoever to you receiving this inheritance, and that they were legally bound to contact you and invite you to a meeting in their offices at a certain time and date for the reading of the last Will and Testament of their deceased client. The Attorney went on to inform you that to receive this massive fortune, it was required of you to come and to be physically present of the reading of the last Will and Testament of your deceased relative, and you must be willing to accept the terms and conditions outlined in this Will, and then they would be legally bound to convey to you the full inheritance that is now yours, in accordance with the terms and conditions outlined in the legal documents. Now, would you be willing to go to that meeting? Do you think that you would change your schedule if necessary to be present at this reading of this Will and all the details

God's Will

concerning your vast inheritance and the wealth that is now yours?

Yes, I believe we all would do whatever is necessary to be present at that gathering, and to listen very carefully at the reading of the Will and all the details necessary for you to receive what is now legally yours for the taking.

But, if you didn't believe the Attorney that called you, or, if you really didn't believe that they would give you your inheritance, or if you chose not to believe you are a legal co-heir, then; I suppose you wouldn't bother to go, and you certainly would not be concerned with the untold wealth that is yours. So, I guess, whoever happened to show-up would get it all.

Well, the book we call the *Holy Bible* is the last Will and Testament of the Owner and Creator of the universe, and it has two parts; the Old Testament and the New Testament. If you are a born-again believer, then you are a legal co-heir to the Kingdom of God. (Romans 8:17) To make any attempt to measure, or even imagine the vast riches and immense wealth that are included within the Kingdom of God would be a monumental task, but; praise God, our good, good Father has it all written down for us to read, study, and discover what is ours as heirs and co-heirs with Christ.

The Word of God is the will of God for His children, and everything in the whole universe is His, and it is His good pleasure to give it all to His children (Luke 12:32). So, the only person that can keep you from discovering and receiving your full inheritance is you through simple unbelief and/or being too lethargic to read and study the Father's will and all His great promises. We must then become a doer of the word (James 1:22), not just a hearer, deceiving ourselves.

I find it very sad when I hear someone say, "Gosh, I sure wish I knew what God's will is for my life? I pray and ask, but; I never get an answer."

Well, I really don't know how to reply to that person because they obviously do not believe the *Holy Bible* is God's Word, and they apparently do not believe that the Bible is God's will for them and for all that will believe and receive. God's will for you and I is not a secret, He wrote it down for us! Our question is this: Why won't people read and study the Word?

Why would God give you, me, or anyone else additional instructions if we have not bothered to study, believe, and at least made some effort to apply the instructions that He has already written down for all His children to build their lives upon. And we are not just referring to the unchurched folks here. No, all we need to do is look around a bit to see how people who claim to be Christians are living to understand that many of these people clearly do not believe the Bible is the Truth, because they would not be living the way they are if they really believed that God's Word is God's will for us to apply to our day-to-day lives.

Our faith life is a relationship with the One who gave it all, so we could be in a relationship with Him. So, if we really believe that our faith life is all about relationship, then tell me; how can you have a relationship with someone that you never spend any time with? The sad truth is that many people know some stuff about God, and do not know Him. And the things that they think they know has come mostly from things they have heard others say about Him, and not from personal experience. The written Word is the primary way everyone begins their relationship with our Lord, and as we read and meditate on His Word, it comes alive in our spirits.

Our Bible contains thirty-nine books in the Old Testament and twenty-seven books in the New Testament. The Old Testament (the Hebrew Bible) is comprised of three components referred to as Teachings, Prophets, and Writings. The first five books of the Old Testament are often referred to as the Torah or the Law, and this is what is called the Teachings. Within the Torah are six hundred thirteen specific commands and if you included the Prophets and the Writings there are literally thousands more oracles, precepts, and commands within those books. Moving to the New Testament, there are close to one thousand specific commands for us to study. There are several Bible scholars and theologians that would debate with you the exact number of commands within our Bible, but; that is not what we wish to do or is that the purpose of this book. Instead, we hope to simplify all this because being a Jesus follower is not about rules and regulations, it's about relationship.

This dissertation is not intended to convince you that the Bible is the inspired Word of God. The assumption we have made is that you believe the complete Bible from Genesis to Revelation is the whole counsel of God, and it contains God's will for all of mankind, and for all time, and for all generations.

With that in mind, we shall next proceed to the Scriptures that radically simplify all of these promises, commands, and precepts within the Word, and this notion of knowing and "doing" or applying the will of God to our daily life, because we must: Be doers of the word and not hears only, deceiving yourselves. James 1:22 MEV

So, in our next chapter; we shall look at what our Lord Jesus has said and done because God's Word is God's will for our lives, and we know that this is true because Jesus said repeatedly that He only came to do the Fathers will and He only said what He heard His Father say and He only did what He saw His Father do. So, to state this another way, whatever Jesus said and did was and is the will of our heavenly Father God.

Therefore, we must submit to Jesus, our great Shepherd and High Priest; in order that we might live spiritually fruitful lives at peace with God and man, thus fulfilling Father God's plans and purposes of bringing His children to full maturity, which means being progressively transformed into the image of Jesus. This is God's will for you and me.

Now may the God of peace [Who is the Author and the Giver of peace], Who brought again from among the dead our Lord Jesus, that great Shepherd of the sheep, by the blood [that sealed, ratified] the everlasting agreement (covenant, testament), strengthen (complete, perfect) and make you what you ought to be and equip you with everything good that you may carry out His will; [while He Himself] works in you and accomplishes that which is pleasing in His sight, through Jesus Christ (the Messiah); to Whom be the glory forever and ever (to the ages of the ages). Amen (so be it). Hebrews 13:20-21 AMPC

This is the Believer's Mandate.

Chapter Seven

Love

Foundational Truth: God is love, and the greatest commandment is love.

One day Jesus was teaching and the Sadducees and the Pharisees (the religious bunch) were up to their regular manipulative games of trying to trip-up Jesus and catch Him saying something that they could use to accuse Him of some transgression of the Torah. These men were the religious Jewish leaders and the so-called experts of the Law. Let's see how Jesus responded to their questioning. The passages we will be examining can be found in Matthew 22:34-40, Mark 12:28-31, and Luke 10:25-28, and we shall look at all three for our study because Jesus told us that all the oracles, precepts, revelations, and commandments contained in the Bible can be summarized into these two commands that are outlined in these Scriptures, and contained within these commands, is the answer to eternal life. Wow!

When the Pharisees heard that He silenced the Sadducees, they came together. One of them, who was a lawyer, tested Him by asking Him, Teacher, which is the greatest commandment in the Law? Jesus answered him, You shall love the Lord your God with all your heart, and with all your soul, and with all your mind. This is the first and great commandment. And the second is like it: You shall love your neighbor as yourself. On these two commandments hang all the Law and the Prophets. Matthew 22:34-40 MEV

One of the scribes came and heard them reasoning together. Perceiving that Jesus had answered them well, he ask Him, Which is the first commandment of all? Jesus answered him, The first of all the commandments is, Hear O Israel, the Lord our God is one Lord. You shall love the Lord your God with all your heart, and with all your soul, and with all your mind, and with all your strength. This is the first commandment. The second is this: You shall love your neighbor as yourself. There is no other commandment greater than these. Mark 12:28-31 MEV

Love

Now, a lawyer stood up and tested Him, saying, Teacher, what must I do to inherit eternal life? He said to him, What is written in the Law? How do you read? He answered, You shall love the Lord your God with all your heart, and with all your soul, and with all your strength, and with all your mind and your neighbor as yourself. He said to him, You have answered correctly. Do this, and you will live. Luke 10:25-28 MEV

We just read that Jesus said that this command is the greatest of all the commandments:

Hear, O Israel: The Lord is our God. The Lord is One! And you shall love the Lord your God with all your heart and with all your soul and with all your might. Deuteronomy 6:4-5 MEV

And Jesus said this Scripture is the second greatest commandment in the Word of God:

You shall not take vengeance, nor bear any grudge against the children of your people, but you shall love your neighbor as yourself: I am the Lord. Leviticus 19:18 MEV

In summary, Jesus said you must love the Lord with all that you are: spirit, soul, and body; and you must love others, just as you love yourself. This is a synopsis of the whole Bible and all its precepts and commandments. Love God and love others. Can it really be this simple?

To begin to understand this awesome command from our Lord, we must begin with the word "love" as used in the Gospels. As we know, the New Testament was written in the Greek language and the word in these verses that has been translated "love" in our English translations is the Greek word *Agape*.

One of the things we really appreciate about the Greek language is its depth and detail. This is a very good example of this added depth when we come to this word "love."

In our humble opinion, this is one of the most abused, distorted, and miscomprehended words in the English language and in our culture today. As an example of this on any given day in our interactions with others, you might hear someone say "Oh, I love those shoes" or "I love my Mom" or "I love my job" or "I love pizza" or "I love my kids" or "I love my dog" or "I love walking on the beach" or "I love my wife" or "I love my car" or "I love dancing" or end a conversation with "love ya" or a hundred other examples we all see and hear every day.

Come on now, do we really value our children on the same level as shoes or pizza? Or do we love our mom and our kids, and our spouse equally and in the same way? Of course not. Nonetheless we are all guilty of abusing the word "love" to the point that we have diminished its worth and many are not even sure what it means anymore. One thing is for sure, we need a fresh revelation of the *agape* love of God and how are we to *agape* love Him in obedient response with our whole being: spirit, soul, and body.

There are four words commonly used in modern Greek language for love. We are not going to do an exhaustive word study here, but; a cursory synopsis to help us understand the contrast between the diverse kinds or types of love and the love of God or God's kind of love, which is perfect, unconditional, and unending.

Storge – (Used 3 times in the New Testament) Devoted affection or natural obligation towards parents, children, kindred, dog, or other close family relationship. Loyal, honoring, dedication to someone or something. When this word is used with the "a" prefix it means devoid or without this kind or type of love. (Scripture references: Romans 1:31, II Timothy 3:3, Romans 12:10)

Phileo – (Used 25 times in the New Testament) Affectionate fondness regarding a person or object. Taking pleasure in a person, place, or thing. A giving and receiving brotherly love. (Scripture references: Matthew 6:5, Mark 14:44, Luke 20:46, John 11:3, John 12:25, Titus 3:15, Revelation 22:15)

Eros – (This word is not in the Scriptures) Erotic, sexual passion/attraction. Self-satisfaction, self-serving kind of love. A love that is an emotional love based on lust/chemistry. This love says: *I love you because you make me happy and make me feel good.* This love basically gives because it is looking for what it can receive. If it fails to get what it wants or expects, this so-called love turns into resentment and/or bitterness and it says: *I don't love you anymore.* This love is codependent upon being attractive in some way, such as physical attractiveness, pleasure, influence, money, prestige, etc. to another person. This is a conditional type of love. This word is not used in the New Testament or The Septuagint, however; it is the name of the Greek god of love that the pagans worshiped.

Agape – (Used 320 times in the New Testament as follows: *Agape* noun 116x, *Agapao* verb 143x, *Agapetos* adjective 61x) The highest, greatest, finest, most noble, honest expression of love. Unconditional, empathetic, sacrificial, totally submitted love. To esteem, respect, and highly value others more than self. To be the ultimate giver of absolute unconditional love. This should be the consuming passion for the true follower of Jesus Christ. This is the God-kind of love. This love cannot and will not fail. (Scripture references: Matthew 6:24, Matthew 22:37, Matthew 24:12, Mark 10:21, Luke 6:27, Luke 6:32, Luke 6:35, Luke 11:42, John 5:42, John 14:15, John 17:23, Romans 5:5, Romans 5:8, Romans 8:28, Romans 8:35, Romans 8:39, Romans 13:10, I Corinthians 13:1-13, Ephesians 5:1-2, Hebrews 12:6, James 1:12, Revelation 1:5, Revelation 12:11)

Some selected passages of Scripture that agape is used twenty times and capture the essence of the *agape* love of Father God:

For God so loved the world that He gave His only begotten Son, that whoever believes in Him should not perish, but have eternal life. John 3:16 MEV

Beloved, let us love one another, for love is of God, and everyone who loves is born of God, and knows God. Anyone who does not love does not know God, for God is love. In this way the love of God was revealed to us, that God sent His only begotten Son into the world, that we might live through Him. In this is love: not that we loved God, but that He loved us and sent His Son to be the atoning sacrifice for our sins. Beloved, if God so loved us, we must also love one another. No one has seen God at any time. If we love one another, God dwells in us, and His love is perfected in us. I John 4:7-12 MEV

A new commandment I give to you, that you love one another, even as I have loved you, that you also love one another. By this all men will know that you are My disciples, if you have love for one another. John 13:34-35 MEV

A new commandment? Jesus had already said we are to love our neighbor as ourselves. So, what exactly is new here? Jesus said I am now commanding you to love *agape* one another (your brothers and sisters in Christ) just as I have loved *agape* you. Jesus said this is how the world will be able to identify that you are My true followers is this agape love that you have for one another. Is not Jesus again commanding us to imitate Him? So, we now know what our measuring stick is if we can answer this question. How did Jesus agape love us?

To begin to answer that question, may we now first contemplate the centricity of Christ. Jesus our Lord is the absolute epicenter of everything in the universe and our lives as His followers.

[The Father] has delivered and drawn us to Himself out of the control and the dominion of darkness and has transferred us into the kingdom of the Son of His love. In Whom we have our redemption through His blood, [which means] the forgiveness of our sins. [Now] He is the exact likeness of the unseen God [the visible representation of the invisible]; He is the Firstborn of all creation. For it was in Him that all things were created, in heaven and on earth, things seen and things unseen, whether thrones, dominions, rulers, or authorities; all things were created and exist through Him [by His service, intervention] and in and for Him. And He Himself existed before all things, and in Him all things consist (cohere, are held together). He also is the Head of [His] body, the church; seeing He is the Beginning, the Firstborn from among the dead, so that He alone in everything and in every respect might occupy the chief place [stand first and be preeminent]. For it pleased [the Father] that all the divine fullness (the sum total of the divine perfection, powers, and attributes) should dwell in Him permanently. And God purposed that through (by the service, the intervention of) Him [the Son] all things should be completely reconciled back to Himself, whether on earth or in heaven, as through Him, [the Father] made peace by means of the blood of His cross.

And although you at one time were estranged and alienated from Him and were of hostile attitude of mind in your wicked activities, yet now has [Christ, the Messiah] reconciled [you to God] in the body of His flesh through death, in order to present you holy and faultless and irreproachable in His [the Father's] presence. [And this He will do] provided that you continue to stay with and in faith [in Christ], well-grounded and settled and steadfast, not shifting or moving away from the hope [which rests on and is inspired by] the glad tidings (the Gospel), which you heard and which has been preached [as being designed for and offered without restrictions] to every person under heaven, and of which [Gospel] I, Paul, became a minister. Colossians 1:13-23 AMPC

Jesus, the only begotten Son, the Master and Creator of the universe, in absolute total submission to His Father's will, freely stripped Himself of all His splendor, majesty, power, dominion, and glory and came to this wicked and deprived planet as a helpless baby born in a barn, to suffer hunger, thirst, insults, torment, ridicule, rejection, pain, mental anguish, torture, shame, and total humiliation at the hands of those He created, and to die the cruelest death imaginable, even death on a Roman cross, fashioned from

Love

a tree that He spoke into existence, and to literally become a curse for us, and to die and literally go to hades, just so He could then confront satan and all the demons in hades, and to utterly defeat all the powers of darkness, and thus He overcome death, hell, and the grave, to then be resurrected and restored and returned to glory at the right hand of the Father, taking with Him as He ascended all the righteous souls waiting in Sheol. (Psalm 49:15, 86:13)

Jesus willingly did all of this because of love. Jesus loves you, and He did all of this to pay our ransom debt that we could not pay, and to become the way for us to be reconciled back to the Father, so we can be washed and forgiven for all our sins, so we can now spend all eternity with Him in His presence. This is how Jesus agape loved us. He laid-down His life to give us life; and this is now our pattern to follow.

God is love. The greatest commandment is love. The Believer's Mandate is love. Each one of us is commanded to love Jesus and to love others. This is the answer to the question: Why am I here? We are here to learn to love.

So, here in the real world, what does this look like? How do we do this? How do we learn to love God and

The Believer's Mandate

others with our whole being? How do we love God with our spirit, soul,

and body; twenty-four hours a day, seven days a week, and three hundred sixty-five days a year? How do we truly love others with this God-kind of agape love? The only way we can do this is by and through our supernatural Helper, the Holy Spirit; as we are fully committed and surrendered to following Jesus.

This is the Believer's Mandate.

Chapter Eight

What about the rich guy

Foundational Truth: We must deny ourselves and take up our cross and follow Jesus.

Jesus was commissioning His twelve disciples and launching them out on their first ministry training mission two-by-two. He gave them power and authority to preach the Gospel of the kingdom of God, and to heal the sick, cleanse the lepers, raise the dead, and cast out demons. These were the things that they had seen Jesus do, and now He was commanding them to go and imitate what they had seen Him do. He sent them out as disciples, but they returned apostles. Jesus taught His disciples many things, but; let's look at specifically what Jesus said about their (and our) commitment level and priorities.

Do not think that I have come to bring peace upon the earth; I have not come to bring peace, but a sword. For I have come to part asunder a man from his father, and a daughter from her mother, and a newly married wife from her mother-in-law; And a man's foes will be they of his own household. He who loves [and takes more pleasure in] father or mother more than [in] Me is not worthy of Me; and he who loves [and takes more pleasure in] son or daughter more than [in] Me is not worthy of Me; And he who does not take up his cross and follow Me [cleaving steadfastly to Me, conforming wholly to My example in living and, if need be, in dying also] is not worthy of Me. Matthew 10:34-38 AMPC

And He said to all, If any person wills to come after Me, let him deny himself [disown himself, forget, lose sight of himself and his own interests, refuse and give up himself] and take up his cross daily and follow Me [cleave steadfastly to Me, conform wholly to My example in living and, if need be, in dying also]. For whoever would preserve his life and save it will lose and destroy it, but whoever loses his life for My sake, he will preserve and save it [from penalty of eternal death]. For what does it profit a man, if he gains the whole world and ruins or forfeits (loses) himself? Because whoever is ashamed of Me and of My teachings, of him will the Son of Man be ashamed when He comes in the [threefold] glory (the splendor and majesty) of Himself and of the Father and of the holy angels. Luke 9:23-26 AMPC

And at another time, as Jesus was addressing a multitude, He taught the people about the personal cost, commitment level, and the raw requirements of discipleship.

Now huge crowds were going along with [Jesus], and He turned and said to them, If anyone comes after Me and does not hate his [own] father and mother [in the sense of indifference to or relative disregard for them in comparison with his attitude toward God] and [likewise] his wife and children and brothers and sisters - [yes] and even his own life also - he cannot be My disciple. Whoever does not persevere and carry his own cross and come after (follow) Me cannot be My disciple. So then, any of you who does not forsake (renounce, surrender claim to, give up, say good-bye to) all that he has cannot be My disciple. Luke 14:25-27,33 AMPC

I have heard some Bible teachers say that this phraseology "take up his cross and follow Me" is a Jewish idiom, and not meant to be taken literally. We must respectfully, but completely; disagree because the Greek word *Stauros* is used twenty-seven times throughout the New Testament and is translated to the English word "cross" twenty-seven times. *Stauros* means cross-beam, or the crosspiece of the Roman cross. The Roman government crucified the worst criminals on these wooden crosses, completely naked; and in public places for all to see. This cruel and humiliating form of capital punishment was reserved for those that were not Roman citizens, hence; everything about the practice was totally appalling and repulsive to the Jewish people. Therefore, we do not believe that referring to the cross would have been something that Jesus or any other Jewish person would have used in their day-to-day communications with other Jewish friends and/or kindred. No, this would be a clarion call to take up a burden against your own will or desire and bear it as far as it is required, even to your death, if need be.

So, what exactly did Jesus want to communicate to us? The wooden cross-beam was the burden of the individual to carry as they make their way to the place of sacrifice, and to "pick-up your cross" you must first put down and leave whatever is in your hands to carry the cross.

What About The Rich Guy

What Jesus means is that you must "deny yourself" and that you must surrender your plans as you submit to following Jesus, even if that means physically dying, as some have in the past, and many more will in the future; in these last days. To be a true follower, or disciple of Jesus means to become just like Jesus in every way. We must deny ourselves: which means to die to our flesh-man. Take up our cross: Which means to die to our soul-man. And then we can follow Jesus: Which means to be led by the Holy Spirit.

If this is the first time you have ever really considered these commands of Jesus, then this teaching probably seems a bit radical to you right now, but please hang-in there with us as we continue our search for the Truth.

Here are a few hard questions we must ask ourselves. Am I willing to follow Jesus even if it costs me most of my friends? Am I willing to follow Jesus if my family disowns me? Am I willing to follow Jesus even if I become estranged from my own children and family? What if it costs me my inheritance? What if it ruins my reputation? What if I lose my position of influence? My hobbies? My possessions? My job? My career? What if I lost my freedom? What if I were thrown into jail? What if it cost me my life? Here is the bottom line:

Are the things you are currently living for, worth Jesus dying for? Selah.

To become a true disciple of Jesus Christ demands that you must willingly surrender all your plans, dreams, hobbies, interests, and pursuits because you are no longer the lord of your life. Jesus will not share His throne with anyone or anything. Nothing can be placed before or above your absolute trust and complete devotion to Jesus.

Therefore, this is the reason that Paul, Peter, James, Jude, Timothy, and John all identified themselves or were called a *doulos* in the Greek, which is translated most literally as bond-servant of the Lord Jesus Christ. (Romans 1:1, II Peter 1:1, James 1:1, Jude 1:1, II Timothy 2:24, Revelation 1:1) A servant no longer has their own plans and pursuits because they live only to serve and fulfill their master's will, just as Jesus, our living example and our Master, came to fulfill His Father's will.

Next, let's look at some additional examples of these principals in the Truth book, such as the encounter with the "rich, young, ruler" recorded in the synoptic Gospel's of Matthew 19:16-30, Mark 10:17-31, and Luke 18:18-30. As we have suggested before, this account is important enough to be included in all three

What About The Rich Guy

of the eye witness's writings, therefore; worthy of very careful consideration and study, but; for our purposes, we shall focus on the details we find in Mark's Gospel.

When He set out on His way, a man came running and knelt before Him, and asked Him, Good Teacher, what must I do to inherit eternal life? He said to him, Why do you call Me good? No one is good, except God alone. You know the commandments, Do not commit adultery, Do not murder, Do not steal, Do not bear false witness, Do not defraud, Honor your father and mother. He answered Him, Teacher, all these have I observed from my youth. Mark 10:17-20 MEV

We have learned from reading the three different Gospel accounts that this individual was a very wealthy and "Rich" individual, and he was a healthy, youthful man in the prime of his life, thus being described as "Young", and he held a position of power, influence, and legal authority over others in Israel making him a "Ruler" and known among the people.

This Rich Young Ruler was most likely a member of the Great Sanhedrin, or at the very least a member of the local Synagogue Council, and his political aspirations most likely included plans to be accepted as part of this exclusive group of leaders.

The Great Sanhedrin and the government of Israel.

We have referenced the Great Sanhedrin or the Council, in chapter four and here in chapter eight and again in chapter ten and eleven to follow. We all need to have at least a basic yet fundamental understanding of what the Sanhedrin was and how it came to be, and who were its members to fully understand the culture and the governance of the people during the first century AD during the earthly ministry of Jesus and during the early developmental years of the Church because there are more than twenty references in the Gospels and in Acts to this group of people.

So, we shall provide a summation of its function and an outline description of the members of the Council or Sanhedrin here for our learning. First, we must locate the beginning of this Council within the Scriptures.

Then the Lord said to Moses, Gather to Me seventy men of the elders of Israel, whom you know to be elders of the people, and officers over them, and bring them to the tent of meeting, that they may take a stand there with you. And I will come down, and I will take of the Spirit which is on you and will put it on them, and they will bear the burden of the people with you, and you will not bear it by yourself. Numbers 11:16-17 MEV

What About The Rich Guy

    This is widely accepted by most Bible scholars as the origination of the Council of seventy or the Sanhedrin. You can read further about the duties and responsibilities of these men as appointed rulers and judges over the people during the forty years in the wilderness in Exodus chapter 18. Moses was the God appointed leader of the people, however; Moses' authority was delegated to this group of seventy others to lead, guide, and judge among the entire nation of Israel, but; the final word on any matter came back to Moses. (Other Scriptures for further study: II Chronicles 19:4-11, Ezra 6:7-8, Jeremiah 26:7-17, Ezekiel 8:11-12)

    Now advancing through time more than twelve centuries to the first century AD, the Great Sanhedrin or the Supreme Council consisted of seventy members plus one. The one additional member was the current High Priest in Israel, and he served as the Council's president.

    This body was constructed of three sub-groups. The first sub-group were the chief priests, of which there were 24 divisions of the Aaronic priesthood, as established during the reign of King David (see I Chronicles 24), and the second sub-group were the 24 elders or rulers of the people or tribal chiefs of the numerous clans and family groups among the Israelites, and the third sub-group were 22 scribes or lawyers which were the experts, teachers, and the transcribers of the sacred Scriptures. During the Temple years, (until 70 AD) this group assembled every day in the Temple court except for the Lord's Feasts and festival days and Sabbath days. A legal quorum was one third or twenty-three members physically present to rule. Again, the Great Sanhedrin was constituted of twenty-four chief priests, twenty-four elders, and twenty-two scribes, equaling the seventy-member Supreme Council.

Jesus referred to the religious members of the Sanhedrin in Matthew 23 and their corruption. Of course, we see reference to the Sanhedrin over and over linked to Jesus' so-called trials: The chief priests and the elders and the entire Sanhedrin searched for false witness against Jesus to put Him to death, but they found none. Yes, though many false witnesses came forward, they found none. Matthew 26:59-60 MEV (see also Matthew 26:57-68, Mark 14:53-65, Mark 15:1-2, Luke 22:54-71, Luke 23:1-5, John 18:12-34, John 19:6-21)

You can also see recorded in the book of Acts the persecution of the apostles and the believers by the Great Sanhedrin for decades. (see Acts 4, 5, 6, 7, 8, 9, 22, 23)

What About The Rich Guy

Some of the more specific members of the Great Sanhedrin identified in the Scriptures included, Annas and Caiaphas, Rabbi Gamaliel, Saul of Tarsus, Nicodemus, Joseph of Arimathea, and the Rich Young Ruler.

To be a viable candidate under consideration for one of the very limited appointments to the Sanhedrin, the man must be established and known as being an accepted fellow of one of these three sub-groups and you also must have been a member of your local Council or the lesser Sanhedrin first. Each village or community throughout Israel would have a lesser Sanhedrin that would have had a maximum of 23 members that gathered at the local Synagogue and/or at the gate to the city to judge or rule on local matters. The base requirement for this local Council to rule on any matter was a minimum of ten members present, which constituted a legal quorum. (see Ruth 4:1-12)

Further prerequisites for the potential candidates, and for all the existing selected members of Great Sanhedrin were: One must have been educated in the Scriptures and must speak and read multiple languages fluently. One must have been born as a legitimate (not born out of wedlock) offspring of Jewish parents, and must be in good health, without any physical infirmity, flaw or blemish. One must possess an excellent reputation, be a man of influence, and be highly esteemed by all. He must be the Chief man of his tribe, and the husband to one wife, and must be very wealthy.

To be ordained as a "Rabbi with authority" during the first century AD in Israel, the individual would have been nominated for ordination by the sitting High Priest and thus under the authority of the Great Sanhedrin. This is exactly why the priests and scribes and the religious gang questioned Jesus' authority when He taught because He didn't go to them and ask for their permission to preach and teach, thus they didn't understand the anointing upon Jesus nor did they comprehend why or how He taught with such power and authority.

The United States of America was established by our founding fathers on Biblical principles and we believe this is just one of many examples of this Scriptural influence upon the framers and originators of this constitutional republic that says, "In God we trust". We believe the Sanhedrin was the inspiration behind our three sub-groups that constitute the three-branch government of the United States of America;

What About The Rich Guy

the Judicial branch, the Executive branch, and the Legislative branch. Judges, Rulers, and Lawyers.

Now, shall we return to our encounter with the Rich Young Ruler.

We can plainly see here in these Scriptures that this healthy young man came running, kneeling, and addressing Jesus with great reverence as Good Teacher.

A man in the first century did not run unless it was of the utmost importance, such as an emergency; since it was undignified to run because only women, children, and servants ran. Also, we see that this man came before Jesus and knelt before Him. Again, a grown man in that day would have only knelt before someone that was clearly in a much greater position to himself, and he obviously acknowledges that Jesus a very moral and ethical person (good) that was highly educated and wise (teacher). If this rich young ruler was living among us today, we would likely all admire this person because he would appear to be young, attractive, smart, wealthy, influential, important, law abiding, good, humble, respectable, and prosperous person within our community, that lives a very honorable life. We might even go so far to say that it seems that this model citizen must be living under the blessings and the favor of God. It would seem by all measures that this individual would be enjoying an almost ideal life, and on top of all that; his one and only question is about his prospective eternal destination, proving he is a big picture thinker and planning for the future. Wow, this man has got it together. What could possibly be missing in his life?

Then Jesus, looking upon him, loved him and said to him, You lack one thing: Go your way, sell whatever you have and give to the poor, and you will have treasure in heaven. And come, take up the cross and follow Me. He was saddened by that word, and he went away grieving. For he had many possessions. Jesus looked around and said to His disciples, How hard it will be for those who have wealth to enter the kingdom of God! Mark 10:21-23 MEV

Jesus, the Son of God, filled with the Holy Spirit; looked upon him, with great discernment. We might say that He "looked straight through him" right into his heart, and then Jesus loved him. The English word "love" is translated from the Greek word *Agape.*

Jesus discerned this young man's earnest heart condition and saw that he had a serious iniquity problem. Jesus saw that this man was an idolater. Anyone or anything that someone values higher than his love, devotion, and trust in God, that person or possession has become an idol in that person's life, and no idolaters will enter heaven.

Do you not know that the unrighteous will not inherit the kingdom of God? Do not be deceived. Neither the sexually immoral, nor idolaters, nor adulterers, nor male prostitutes, nor homosexuals, nor thieves, nor covetous, nor drunkards, nor revilers, nor extortioners will inherit the kingdom of God. I Corinthians 6:9-10 MEV

Now the works of the flesh are revealed, which are these: adultery, sexual immorality, impurity, lewdness, idolatry, sorcery, hatred, strife, jealousy, rage, selfishness, dissensions, heresies, envy, murders, drunkenness, carousing, and the like. I warn you, as I previously warned you, that those who do such things shall not inherit the kingdom of God. Galatians 5:19-21 MEV

For this you know, that no sexually immoral or impure person, or one who is greedy, who is an idolater, has any inheritance in the kingdom of Christ and of God. Ephesians 5:5 MEV

He who overcomes shall inherit all things, and I will be his God and he shall be My son. But the cowardly, the unbelieving, the abominable, the murderers, the sexually immoral, the sorcerers, the idolaters, and all liars shall have their portion in the lake which burns with fire and brimstone. This is the second death. Revelation 21:7-8 MEV

Blessed are those who do His commandments, that they may have the right to the tree of life, and may enter through the gates into the city. Outside are the dogs and sorcerers, and the sexually immoral and murderers and idolaters and everyone who loves and practices a lie. Revelation 22:14-15 MEV

We must realize and see that if we truly *agape* love someone, we will speak the Truth to them, just like Jesus loved this young man that came to Him and asked what he must do to receive an inheritance in the kingdom age, and go to heaven when his earthly life was over? Would it be loving to not tell the person if they don't change their ways they are headed for absolute disaster and a catastrophic end?

Jesus went on to say to His followers that it was very difficult for a person of worldly wealth and material possessions to enter the kingdom of God. Why?

The disciples were astonished at His words. But Jesus answered again, Children, how hard it is for those who trust in riches to enter the kingdom of God! It is easier for a camel to go through the eye of a needle than for a rich man to enter the kingdom of

God. They were astonished beyond measure, saying among themselves, Who then can be saved? Jesus, looking at them, said, With men it is impossible, but not with God. For with God all things are possible. Mark 10:24-27 MEV

The disciples were *astonished* at His words. This word translated astonished is from the Greek word *Thambeo,* which means to be so utterly amazed, stupefied, or dumbfounded to the point of being emotionally stunned and shut down, even to the point of being terrified.

Then Jesus referred to the largest land animal they had ever seen as an illustrative example and said it would be easier for this huge land animal that would be about seven-foot-tall and more than one thousand pounds to pass through the eye of a sewing needle than a man of worldly wealth to enter the eternal kingdom of heaven.

This new doctrine that Jesus was teaching them at this moment was rocking their world. These men were literally in a state of shock and struggling to comprehend what Jesus was telling them. Up to this point in their lives, many of the legendary and highly revered ancestors, that all were considered mighty men of God were also men of great wealth and influence. Men such as Job, Abraham, Isaac, Jacob, Joseph, David, Solomon, Daniel, the prophets, the kings, and every member of the great Sanhedrin of Israel.

These men had been taught their whole life that great wealth and prosperity was a sign of God's blessing and favor on these men's lives, families, livestock, fruit, and fields. But, now these words of Jesus had them shook-up and mentally battling to process this radical new way of thinking. In their minds, it was probably obvious that this rich, young, member of the Sanhedrin must have been a godly man, walking in the favor of the Lord, and his place in the eternal kingdom must have been secure. And now, Jesus is telling them that this respectable, wealthy, and honored man among their people and nation had a big problem and that he must go and dispossess of all his great wealth and give up his reputation and position in society to inherit eternal life. After this rich, young, ruler leaves distraught, they too begin to question how in the world would they measure up if this man was not going to inherit eternal life.

Therefore, Jesus said to them that it is impossible for a man to be good enough or honorable enough or rich enough to enter the kingdom on his own merits, and that by and through God's grace alone could

What About The Rich Guy

anyone enter His kingdom. Even though Jesus had taught them similar precepts and introduced similar thoughts and concepts before this day, the disciples had not quite assimilated this new Truth yet. This was a significant adjustment to their thinking and beliefs. This is a good example of renewing our minds and repenting, which is changing our thoughts, ideas, and beliefs to line-up with the Truth, not popular opinion or traditions of men.

Peter began to say to Him, Look, we have left everything and have followed You. Jesus answered, Truly I say to you, there is no one who has left a house or brothers or sisters or father or mother or wife or children or fields, for My sake and for the gospel's sake, who shall not receive a hundred times as much now in this age, houses and brothers and sisters and mothers and children and fields, with persecution, and in the age to come, eternal life. But many who are first will be last, and the last first. Mark 10:28-31 MEV

Peter was the spokesman for the disciples and being quite disturbed by this new doctrine said to Jesus "Wow, Master what are we gonna do? We have left behind everything we had already to follow you. We don't have anything more to give. We have walked away from our homes, jobs, and families to be your disciples." Obviously, Jesus wasn't teaching that it is wrong or sinful to possess wealth, but; it is wrong for wealth to possess you. Anything that you trust in other than or before Jesus is an idol. They didn't quite get the connection between this man's unwillingness to sacrifice his wealth and position to follow Jesus as the sin of idolatry and lack of faith, but it is. They also didn't quite get the concept yet that anything that you sacrifice for the sake of advancing the kingdom of God will be returned to you multiplied, and that is exactly why all their esteemed forefathers lived such favored lives because the blessings of God followed their obedience and devotion to God.

The things we give to God may leave our hands, but; those things do not leave our lives. Jesus is teaching that everything we need to fulfill His plans and purposes will be provided into our lives now, but; we should also anticipate troubles to come our way too, nevertheless; we can also expect at the end of our days on earth an inheritance and eternal life, and the question about who would inherit eternal life is what this entire episode was based on to begin with. Let us not miss the major point here. Jesus is asking each of us to deny ourselves and to follow Him first, and by doing so, our rewards will come, but; that the kingdom age works differently that this worldly system in that many individuals that seem to have it all here on earth won't realize that same position in the coming kingdom. Hallelujah!

We know that many people, even those that profess to be a Christian, struggle with this doctrine of self-denial and do not want to believe that it applies to them today, and that somehow this Truth expired or was terminated in some distant past generation. Many want to believe this only applied to first century Christians or that this "take up your cross and follow Me" stuff is just for those special individuals that Jesus calls into vocational ministry to be Evangelists, Pastors, or Missionaries. This is simply not true. The call to follow Jesus was and is for every man, woman, and child - past, present, and future, and especially us, the last days generation that will usher in the King and the age to come.

Jesus was teaching about the last days of the Church age when He said: Truly, I tell you, this generation will not pass away until all these things are fulfilled. Heaven and earth will pass away, but My words will not pass away. Luke 21:32-33 MEV

This means the command to follow Jesus is for you. The call to deny yourself and submit your life

The Believer's Mandate

completely to become a disciple of Jesus is your call. But this money issue can be a real stumbling block to many, and we must get revelation of exactly what the Word teaches about money and the dangers thereof. The old man is dead, so the new man can be led.

This is the Believer's Mandate.

Chapter nine

Money or mammon

Foundational Truth: The love of money is a very serious spiritual problem.

In our last chapter, we were examining the fact that we are all called to discipleship which commands submission of our lives to Jesus and to surrender everything, and we included this Scripture from the Gospel of Luke in chapter eight, but; it bears repeating now as we dig a little deeper into the money thing, but; this time, we'll quote it from *The Message* paraphrase.

One day when large groups of people were walking along with Him, Jesus turned and told them, Anyone who comes to Me but refuses to let go of father, mother, spouse, children, brothers, sisters – yes, even one's own self! – can't be My disciple. Anyone who won't shoulder his own cross and follow behind Me can't be My disciple. Simply put, if you're not willing to take what is dearest to you, weather plans or people, and kiss it good-bye, you can't be My disciple. Luke 14:25-27,33 MSG

Jesus had a lot to say about money and in the passage above Jesus is specifically speaking to the personal cost of discipleship, but; what we must understand is that money and how we deal with money, is a heart or a spiritual issue. A very, very serious spiritual issue. It can literally be a matter of life and death.

No one can serve two masters; for either he will hate the one and love the other, or he will stand by and be devoted to the one and despise and be against the other. You cannot serve God and mammon (deceitful riches, money, possessions, or whatever is trusted in). Matthew 6:24 AMPC

No servant is able to serve two masters; for either he will hate the one and love the other, or he will stand by and be devoted to the one and despise the other, You cannot serve God and mammon (riches, or anything in which you trust and on which you rely). Luke 16:13 AMPC

What is mammon? Mammon is an old Syriac Aramaic word that signifies property, money, possessions, wealth, riches, valuables, worldly goods, or anything loved, coveted, trusted in, admired, or worshipped. It was a common word that was widely used in the first century middle east for worldly wealth.

You adulterers and adulteresses, do you not know that the friendship with the world is enmity with God? Whoever therefore will be a friend of the world is the enemy of God. James 4:4 MEV

The person that would be a servant to mammon would be guilty of the sin described as covetousness, or avariciousness, or idolatry. The servant of mammon would be a friend of the world and the world system, and by default a friend of satan; who is the god of this world. (II Corinthians 4:4) Therefore, this would also position this person as an enemy of God. Let us take a more in-depth look at some specific examples of this sin to see how the Lord deals with this hidden iniquity in the Scriptures.

I would not want you to be unaware that all our fathers were under the cloud, and all passed through the sea, and all were baptized into Moses in the cloud and in the sea; all ate the same spiritual food; and all drank the same spiritual drink, for they drank of that spiritual Rock that followed them, and that Rock was Christ. But many of them God was not well pleased, and they were overthrown in the wilderness. Now these things were our examples to the intent that we should not lust after evil things as they lusted. Neither be idolaters as were some of them. As it is written, The people sat down to eat and drink and rose up to revel. Neither let us commit sexual immorality as some of them committed, when twenty-three thousand fell in one day. Neither let us tempt Christ, as some of them also tempted and were destroyed by serpents. Neither murmur, as some of them also murmured and were destroyed by the destroyer. Now all these things happened to them for examples. They are written as an admonition to us, upon whom the end of the ages has come. Therefore let him who thinks he stands take heed, lest he fall. No temptation has taken you except what is common to man. God is faithful, and He will not permit you to be tempted above what you can endure, but will with the temptation also make a way to escape, that you may be able to bear it. So, my beloved, flee from idolatry. I Corinthians 10:1-14 MEV

We must be very clear here. This passage is from the New Testament and is written as a warning and a rebuke specifically to the Church, which means you and me; not to fall into the same sins that caused the Hebrew children to fall in death in the wilderness, and consequently they did not enter the promised land.

Some folks like to say that the Old Testament does not apply to New Covenant believers today. Well, I must inform those that believe that nonsense that they are deceived. Every writer of the New testament referred to and quoted the Old Testament and Jesus Himself quotes from the Old Testament many, many times, besides the New Testament Scriptures like the one from I Corinthians 10 written above or this one from II Timothy.

But continue in the things that you have learned and have been assured of, knowing those from whom you have learned them, and since childhood you have known the Holy Scriptures, which are able to make you wise unto salvation through the faith that is in Christ Jesus. All Scripture is inspired by God and is profitable for teaching, for reproof, for correction, and for instruction in righteousness, that the man of God may be complete, thoroughly equipped for every good work. II Timothy 3:14-17 (MEV)

What Holy Scriptures do you suppose Apostle Paul was commanding Timothy, and us; to study so that Timothy could be thoroughly equipped for every good work? Of course, Paul was referring to the Old Testament Scriptures because the Hebrew Scriptures were the only inspired Scriptures in existence at that time.

Nevertheless, for those that are stubborn about this Truth, here is another example from one of Paul and Barnabas's large meetings in the city of Antioch of Pisidia, which was built on the slopes of the Taurus Mountains; which was an area notorious for hide-outs of thieves, robbers, and cut-throats of every sort. This might be one reason why young John Mark (Acts 13:13) turned back and returned to his home in Jerusalem.

On the next Sabbath almost the whole city assembled to hear the word of God. But when the Jews saw the crowds, they were filled with jealousy, blaspheming and contradicting what Paul was saying. Then Paul and Barnabas boldly said, It was necessary that the word of God should be spoken to you first. But seeing you reject it, and judge yourselves unworthy of eternal life, we are turning to the Gentiles. For thus has the Lord commanded us: I have established you to be a light of the Gentiles, that you may bring salvation to the ends of the earth. When the Gentiles heard this, they were glad and glorified the word of the Lord. And all who were ordained to eternal life believed. Acts 13:44-48 MEV

Money Or Mammon

Please take note here that recorded in verse 47 Paul says "For thus has the Lord commanded us" and goes on to quote from two Old Testament Scriptures from the book of Isaiah just what the Lord has thus commanded us all, because we are also charged to imitate Paul as it is written: So I implore you, be followers of me. I Corinthians 4:16 MEV (also see I Corinthians 11:1, Philippians 3:17, I Thessalonians 1:6) But, let's review these Scriptures in Isaiah:

I the Lord have called You in righteousness, and will hold Your hand, and will keep You and appoint You for a covenant of the people, for a light of the nations, Isaiah 42:6 MEV

He says, It is a light thing that you should be My servant to raise up the tribes of Jacob and to restore the preserved ones of Israel; I will also make you a light to the nations so that My salvation may reach to the ends of the earth. Isaiah 49:6 MEV

Someone really stiff-necked at this point could say that these two Scriptures were prophesying of Jesus and that person would be exactly correct. However, we are also commanded to follow Jesus Christ in every way. So, we have yet another proof that all Scripture is for every person that professes Jesus as Lord.

Okay, now that we have established that we must study the entire Bible to be wise, to build our faith, to be thoroughly equipped, and to receive the whole council of God, let's go to the book of Joshua chapters 6 & 7 to see yet another prophetic pattern for us to heed.

We would recommend that you read the entire book of Joshua, but; we are going to look at one incident that occurred as Joshua and the Hebrew children were concluding the defeat of the city of Jericho. The city of Jericho prophetically represents the world and the worldly systems.

Jericho was the first city that God instructed Joshua to attack and defeat. God had instructed Joshua that all the silver, gold, bronze, and iron articles within the city were set apart, or dedicated for the Lord. After the overwhelming defeat of Jericho, Joshua sent some men on to the small village of Ai to take it as well.

Joshua's men attacked, and the men of Ai resisted them and ran them off and killed thirty-six of Joshua's men. Well, that was not supposed to happen. Joshua cried out to God and God told him that he had sin in the camp, and that someone had taken some of the things that God said were dedicated to Him. So, Joshua began the process of discovery and learned that a man by the name of Achan had taken and hidden in his tent some of the silver, gold, and raiment of the dedicated items in the city of Jericho that God said were His. Achan had broken the covenant represented by the Ten Commandments that Israel coveted with the Lord. You can't love God and covet things.

Achan answered Joshua and said, Indeed, I sinned against the Lord, the God of Israel. This is what I did: When I saw among the plundered goods a beautiful robe from Babylon, two hundred shekels of silver, and a gold bar weighing fifty shekels, I coveted them, so I took them. They are hidden in the ground in my tent. The silver is underneath them. Joshua 7:20-21 MEV

The approximate value of the silver and gold that Achan coveted and stole from God would be worth about thirty-five thousand dollars today. God instructed Joshua to have Achan and his entire family and his livestock stoned to death and then everything else that he had to be burned. God commanded the Hebrew children to set apart or consecrate the valuables from Jericho, and then Joshua and Israel went on to take the promised land defeating a total of thirty-one kings (Joshua chapter 12) and kingdoms, and God allowed them to keep all the plunder from those thirty kingdoms beyond Jericho. Covetousness is Idolatry and is a very grievous sin in God's sight. This man knew what he was doing was wrong, or he wouldn't have hidden these things in a hole in the ground. Don't be faithless and take what God has asked you to give to Him. Father God will honor your faith and obedience and bless you and those things that concern you.

Therefore put to death the parts of your earthly nature: sexual immorality, uncleanness, inordinate affection, evil desire, and covetousness, which is idolatry. Because of these things, the wrath of God comes on the sons of disobedience. Colossians 3:5-6 MEV

Now, shall we look at the early Church in the book of Acts:

All the believers were of one heart and one soul, and no one said that what he possessed was his own. But to them all things were in common. With great power the apostles testified to the resurrection of the Lord Jesus, and great grace was on them all. There was no one among them who lacked, for all those who were owners of land or houses sold them, and brought the income from what was sold, and placed it at the apostles' feet. And it was distributed to each according to his need. Joseph, whom the apostles called Barnabas (which means, Son of Encouragement), a Levite from the land of Cyprus, sold a field he owned, and brought the money and placed it at the apostles' feet. Acts 4:32-36 MEV

The Temple and the capitol city of Jerusalem.

The Temple was no doubt, the center piece of the nation of Israel and of its capitol city, Jerusalem. The temple complex was a massive and very opulent facility that was roughly one million five hundred thousand square feet. We know that King David collected and personally contributed billions of dollars to the construction fund, and ultimately the total cost of the Temple built by King Solomon in the 10th century BC was well over four hundred billion dollars in today's values. This temple was destroyed by King Nebuchadnezzar, king of Babylon, in 587 BC on the 9th day of the Jewish month of Av. Ezra completed rebuilding the temple in 515 BC, and the King Herod expansion project that grew and improved the temple was completed around 25 AD. It has been recorded by various historians that the King Herod enhanced temple was larger and more beautiful than Solomon's temple.

The Ezra/Herod temple was destroyed by the Romans on the 9th day of the Jewish month of Av in 70 AD, and the Jewish historian Josephus was an eye witness to its breach and destruction. More than one million Jews lost their lives in this Roman siege of Jerusalem and its subsequent destruction. Jesus had prophesied the destruction of the temple and Jerusalem as recorded in Matthew 24, Mark 13, and Luke 21. The first century believers all would have been taught all the things Jesus had been preaching and teaching, which would certainly have included His prophecy about the temple destruction and the utter devastation of Jerusalem. We believe therefore the reason why we see in Acts 4:34 where it says "for all those who were owners of land or houses sold them" these early church believers simply believed the prophetic words of Jesus and disposed of their land and properties as they had opportunity. We can certainly learn from the early church members because we know that we too are living in the very last days before the return of our soon coming King.

The fact that all the believers were of one heart and soul is an awesome truth. This is exactly what every believer as part of the church today is called to grow towards and aspire to, is this kind of unity. Our mindsets should also be that nothing we have is ours exclusively, but instead; we are to "hold on loosely" to all things of this world because everything we have is dedicated to the advancement of the kingdom of God. We all should be ready, willing, and able to freely give of anything and everything we have in our possession as we are led to do so by the Holy Spirit.

As true disciples of Jesus Christ we claim no absolute ownership of anything, but; we know all good things are from our heavenly Father and that we are simply overseers of the time, talent, treasure, and material wealth that has been placed under our stewardship. However, we do not believe that we are to propagate the doctrine that says that everyone is supposed to sell everything he/she has and give the proceeds to the local church. Every one of us has something to offer the body of Christ, as each of us is led to do so, as we see outlined in the Scriptures.

For just as we have many parts in one body, and not all parts have the same function, so we, being many, are one body in Christ, and all are parts of one another. We have diverse gifts according to the grace that is given to us: if prophecy, according to the proportion of faith; if service, in serving; he who teaches, in teaching; he who exhorts, in exhortation; he who gives, with generosity; he who rules, with diligence; he who shows mercy, with cheerfulness. Romans 12:4-8 MEV

Each one of us has been given gifts, talents, and abilities and those gifts are to be used to glorify Jesus and to strengthen His church here on earth. We believe that the Holy Spirit highlighted this example of sacrificial giving as a contrast to the next example we shall see following in Acts chapter five. We also know from Scripture that Barnabas was called into vocational ministry as a missionary. (see Acts 13:1-3) We know and can testify from firsthand experiences, that Jesus still calls and commissions some individuals to sell or give away all their material possessions and go to the mission fields, but; it is wisdom to be certain you have confirmation of this calling before you do any such thing. However, we must consider carefully the matter of Ananias and Sapphira in the early days of the Church.

Now a man named Ananias, with his wife Sapphira, sold a piece of property. He kept back part of the proceeds with his wife's knowledge, and brought a part of it and placed it at the apostles' feet. Then Peter said, Ananias, why has Satan filled your heart to deceive the Holy Spirit and keep back part of the proceeds of the land? While it remained unsold, was it not your own? And when it was sold, was it not under your authority? Why have you conceived this deed in your heart? You did not lie to men, but to God. On hearing these words, Ananias fell down and died. And great fear came on all those who heard these things. The young men rose and wrapped him up and carried him out and buried him. About three hours later his wife came in, not knowing what had happened. Peter said to her, Tell me whether you sold the land for this amount? She said, Yes, for that much. Peter said to her, How is it that you have agreed together to test the Spirit of the Lord? Look! The feet of those who have buried your husband are at the door, and they will carry you out. At once she fell down at his feet and died. Upon entering, the young men found her dead and carried her out and buried her beside her husband. Great fear came on the entire church and on all those who heard these things. Acts 5:1-11 MEV

The only way to interpret the Bible accurately is with the Bible itself, and the Scriptures in Joshua 6 & 7 establishes how the Lord views things that have been dedicated to Him and those people that are covetous idolaters. We can see clearly that this married couple intended to deceive the Church leadership by holding on to some portion of the proceeds of this property transaction, which means that they allowed everyone to believe that they were selling this property to give all of the proceeds to the Church. Furthermore, this act demonstrates their lack of faith in the Lord to provide for their needs, and their hypocrisy in that they were pretending to be more pious than they really were, and of course their deceit proves they were liars. So, to summarize; Ananias and Sapphira were deceitful, lying, hypocritical, idolaters looking for the praise and honor of men. I also personally believe that God was sending a very clear message to His people about how He views this sort of iniquity, again not dissimilar to the Achan incident.

We can also see in the Scriptures that the only people during the earthy ministry of Jesus that He ever publicly chastised and rebuked by proclaimed woes over them and openly confronted their sin and iniquities were: the religious Jews for their hypocrisy (Matthew 23:1-36), and the deceitful moneychangers He drove out of the temple (Luke 19:45-46), and the unbelieving liars (John 8:39-47).

There is another element of this passage we must speak about here before we move on. There are some in the Church today that are teaching a doctrine that has been labeled the "hyper grace" message which basically says that we are under God's unlimited grace and it is unnecessary to repent for our sins because Christ's sacrifice covers all our sins; past, present, and future. The hyper grace message would say that

Ananias and Sapphira were not part of the local church and hence not covered by grace and that is why the Holy Spirit took them out.

We must disagree with this view simply because in the Scriptures we are informed that when this occurred: Great fear came on the entire church and on all those who heard these things. Acts 5:11 MEV

One must ask this question: If Ananias and Sapphira were not church members then why would this event bring great fear on the entire church? The apostle Paul wrote this command in the epistle to the Church at Rome: Therefore consider the goodness and severity of God – severity toward those who fell, but goodness toward you, if you continue in His goodness. Otherwise, you also will be cut off. Romans 11:22 MEV

Our heavenly Father is holy and He has called His children to be holy (I Peter 1:14-15), and in Revelation chapters 2 & 3 in the seven letters to the seven churches in Asia minor, Jesus repeatedly commands us (the Church) to turn away from and repent of our sinful behavior!

To conclude this Truth about worldly wealth and how it is a heart/spiritual issue, let us turn to the epistle of instruction to Timothy and us: But godliness with contentment is great gain. For we brought nothing into this world, and it is certain that we can carry nothing out. If we have food and clothing, we shall be content with these things, but those who desire to be rich fall into temptation and a snare and into many foolish and harmful lusts, which drown men in ruin and destruction. For the love of money is the root of all evil. While coveting after money, some have strayed from the faith and pierced themselves through with many sorrows. I Timothy 6:6-10 MEV

Money itself is an inanimate object, but the love of money is the root of all evil when we put our trust in it, thus this thing has become an Idol or mammon. That is why Jesus said you cannot serve God and mammon. If you are not serving God, then by default you are serving evil, or in other words; you have become a servant of Satan and of his worldly system, the other fallen angels, and the unclean spirits under his control. Whether that was your intent or not doesn't matter, because there is not a third option here. We all serve to one or the other, and the clear command is to submit everything to Jesus our Lord. This is the Believer's mandate. For the Lord is our Judge, the Lord is our Lawgiver, the Lord is our King; He will save us. Isaiah 33:22 AMPC

But, what about the so-called prosperity message that we hear a lot of fuss about these days? We must know in our knower that Jesus is our provider and we are His stewards.

This is the Believer's Mandate.

Chapter Ten

No lack

Foundational Truth: We have the same promises and the same requirements and access to the same supply house that God Almighty promised the richest man that has ever lived.

We shall now provide a cursory review of the life of the original Prosperity Preacher.

This is an expression we hear tossed about in Christendom these days to identify a certain preacher, coupled along with the equally popular "prosperity gospel" moniker to describe his or her message. This terminology seems to hold conflicting implications, some positive and some negative; all depending on which specific faith stream or camp you might choose to be aligned with. But even if the mere mention of this term doesn't quicken your senses, surely at least you have heard and are familiar with this descriptive language and these popular identifiers being widely used within the Church at large today.

We do not desire to enter into or propagate this discussion, but; instead we shall endeavor to study the Scriptures that record first and perhaps the most famous prosperity preacher that has ever lived. Our goal is to seek revelation from the Word of God about these matters and how we might apply these lessons to our own lives and how this impacts the Believer's mandate.

Whom is it that might hold this auspicious title? None other than King Solomon.

The young man Solomon was chosen, named, and prophesied by God to be the third king of all of Israel. (I Chronicles 22:9, I Chronicles 28:5, I Chronicles 29:1)

The fact that Solomon was Divinely named before his birth by God Almighty Himself places Solomon in a very exclusive club of eight: (Ishmael - Genesis 16:11, Isaac - Genesis 17:19, Solomon - I Chronicles 22:9, Josiah - I Kings 13:2, Maher-Shalal-Hash-Baz - Isaiah 8:1-3, Cyrus - Isaiah 44:28, John the Baptist - Luke 1:13, and Jesus - Luke 1:31) Were all these sons Hebrew? Were they all Jewish? Were they all holy men of God? No, they were not, but; what they did have in common is the fact that God has a master plan, and just like these; you are part of His plan and purposes regardless of your heritage or your past. Amen.

Solomon was the second born son of five sons born to Bathsheba, begotten by his renowned father David; the mighty warrior king of all Israel and a man after Father God's own heart. (I Samuel 13:14, I Kings 14:8, Psalm 89:19-37)

And when He had deposed him, He raised up David to be their king; of him He bore witness and said, 'I have found David son of Jesse a man after My own heart, who will do all My will and carry out My program fully.' Acts 13:22 AMPC

According to the Hebrew Scriptures, King David had twenty-one sons from various wives, of which twenty sons are named; along with one daughter named Tamar. Additionally, David sired other numerous and unnamed sons, and possibly daughters; that were born over time of his unknown quantity of concubines. (II Samuel 11:1-12:25, I Chronicles 3:1-9, II Chronicles 11:18)

Preceding his death, King David gave his son Solomon this charge:

I am going the way of all the earth. Be strong, and show yourself to be a man. And keep the charge of the Lord your God, walking in His ways, keeping His statutes, His commandments, His judgements, and His testimonies, as it is written in the Law of Moses, that you may prosper in all that you do and wherever you turn, that the Lord may carry out His word that He spoke concerning me, saying, 'If your children take heed to their way, to walk before Me in faithfulness with all their hearts and with all their souls, you shall not fail to have a man on the throne of Israel.' I Kings 2:2-4 MEV

Early in the commencement years of Solomon's reign, as the control of the kingdom was being firmly established in the hand of Solomon; God Almighty first appeared to Solomon as he represented the nation of Israel and as he was leading those of national influence in sacrificial worship and to seek the Lord.

Now Solomon the son of David strengthened himself over his kingdom, and the Lord his God was with him and made Solomon exceedingly great. And Solomon spoke to all Israel, to the commanders of thousands and of hundreds, to the judges, and to all the leaders in all Israel, the heads of fathers' houses. Then they all went, Solomon and all the assembly that was with him, to the high place that was at Gibeon, because the tent of meeting with God, which Moses the servant of the Lord had made in the wilderness, was there. However, David had brought up the ark of God from Kiriath Jearim to the place he had prepared, for he had pitched a tent for it in Jerusalem. And the bronze altar that Bezalel the son of Uri, the son of Hur, had made was set before the tabernacle of the Lord. And Solomon and the assembly sought it out to seek the Lord. And Solomon went up to the bronze altar before the Lord, which was before the tent of meeting, and he offered up a thousand burnt offerings on it.

So Solomon came from the high place at Gibeon, before the tent of meeting, to Jerusalem, and he reigned over Israel. II Chronicles 1:1-6,13 MEV

The king went to Gibeon to sacrifice there, for that was the great high place, and he offered a thousand burnt offerings on that altar. While he was in Gibeon, the Lord appeared to Solomon in a dream at night, and He said "Ask what you want from Me."

Solomon answered, "You have shown great mercy to Your servant David my father, because he walked before You in faithfulness, righteousness, and uprightness of heart toward You. And You have shown him great kindness in giving him a son to sit on his throne this day. Now, O Lord, my God, You have made Your servant king in place of my father David, and I am still a little child and do not know how to go out or come in. And Your servant is in the midst of Your people whom You have chosen, a great people, so numerous that they cannot be numbered or counted. Give Your servant therefore an understanding heart to judge Your people, that I may discern between good and bad, for who is able to judge among so great a people?"

It pleased the Lord that Solomon had ask this. God said to him, "Because you have asked this and have not asked for yourself long life or riches or the lives of your enemies, but have asked for yourself wisdom so that you may have discernment in judging, I now do according to your words. I have given you a wise and an understanding heart, so that there has never been anyone like you in the past, and there shall never arise another like you. I have also given you what you have not asked, both riches and honor, so that no kings will compare to you all of your days. If you will walk in My ways, keeping My statutes and My commandments as your father David did, then I will lengthen your days."

Solomon awoke and found it was a dream. Then he came to Jerusalem and stood before the ark of the covenant of the Lord and offered up burnt offerings and peace offerings and made a feast for all his servants. I Kings 3:4-15 MEV

In addition to his position as the favored son of King David and being coronated the third monarch of Israel in his early 20's, Solomon was blessed and favored by God to govern while at peace (I Kings 5:4, I Kings 11:42) for most of his forty-year reign – these were the very best and most glorious years in all of Israel's history.

King Solomon was responsible for expanding, controlling, and profiting from the greatest amount of territory in the nation's history (I Kings 4:20-25, II Chronicles 9:26-31), which extended from the great Euphrates River to the north, to the Mediterranean Sea in the west, to the boundary of Egypt to the south.

Solomon was also recognized far and wide for his unequaled wisdom, for being an accomplished author and composer, and for possessing great understanding and immense knowledge of the many and diverse flora and fauna throughout God Almighty's creation. Why would God give a man such wisdom, knowledge, ability, and discernment?

For the very same reason Father God is still giving His creation wisdom and revelation so that absolutely no man has an excuse, or can foolishly claim there is no God; just as the Holy Spirit inspired King David to record:

The [empty-headed] fool has said in his heart, 'There is no God.' They are corrupt, they have done abominable deeds; there is none that does good or right. Psalm 14:1 AMPC

For God's [holy] wrath and indignation are revealed from heaven against all ungodliness and unrighteousness of men, who in their wickedness repress and hinder the truth and make it inoperative. For that which is known about God is evident to them and made plain in their inner consciousness, because God [Himself] has shown it to them. For ever since the creation of the world His invisible nature and attributes, that is, His eternal power and divinity, have been made intelligible and clearly discernible in and through the things that have been made (His handiworks). So [men] are without excuse [altogether without any defense or justification]. Romans 1:18-20 AMPC

King Solomon is accredited with the composition and/or writing of the inspired wisdom books of *Song of Songs, Proverbs*, and *Ecclesiastes*, in our Holy Bible. According to the historical accounts recorded by the ancient Jewish sages, Solomon composed the *Song of Songs* in the first five years or so of his reign as king, and the book of *Proverbs* over the next thirty to thirty-five years of his life, and finally the book of

Ecclesiastes was transcribed during the very last years of Solomon's life and forty-year reign as king of Israel. It is undeniable that the favor and blessings of the Lord was upon David's beloved son Solomon.

The Lord highly exalted Solomon in the sight of all Israel and bestowed on him such royal majesty as had never been on any king in Israel before him. I Chronicles 29:25 MEV

God gave Solomon wisdom and great depth of understanding as well as compassion, as vast as the sand on the seashore. Solomon's wisdom excelled the wisdom of all the people of the East country and all the wisdom of Egypt. For he was wiser than all other men, wiser than Ethan, the Ezrahite, Heman, Kalkol, and Darda, the sons of Mahol; his fame spread throughout all the surrounding nations. He spoke three thousand proverbs, and his songs numbered a thousand and five. He spoke of trees, from the cedar tree that is in Lebanon to the hyssop that springs out of the wall. He also spoke of beasts and of fowl and of insects and fish. People from all over came to hear the wisdom of Solomon, from all kings of the earth, who had heard of his wisdom. I Kings 4:29-34 MEV

However, despite all this acclamation, King Solomon was best known for his vast wealth and the crowning achievement of his lifetime, which was the construction of the magnificent holy temple of God, that was established upon Mount Moriah on the threshing floor property that king David purchased. (I Chronicles 21:18-30)

This place, without doubt the most contested parcel of real estate on earth; was chosen by God Himself to be the eternal capital city of the nation of Israel, and the center of the world; which was, is, and always will be the city of Jerusalem. (Genesis 14:18, Genesis 22:1-14, I Chronicles 6:5-6, Zechariah 2:12, Revelation 21:2)

Before we discuss Solomon's greatest development project of his lifetime, we shall attempt to assemble a synoptic review of his immense personal wealth and influence in geopolitics.

Solomon was the gatekeeper to the major passageways and trade routes utilized by all the various caravans of merchant traders of the day and thus, he controlled the traffic and subsequent flow of goods along these established trade routes that connected the inhabitants of Asia, Africa, and Europe.

King Solomon controlled the land bridge connecting three continents, therefore; Solomon was in position to collect whatever tribute, toll, or duty he deemed appropriate for granting the safe passage of these merchants to transport their wares to their ultimate customer, destination, or marketplace.

The weight of gold that came to Solomon every year was six hundred sixty-six talents of gold. In addition to what the explorers and merchants brought in, all the kings of Arabia and governors of the land brought in gold and silver to Solomon. So King Solomon was greater than all the kings of the earth in wealth and wisdom. II Chronicles 9:13-14,22 MEV

Solomon reigned forty years and received six hundred sixty-six talents of gold each year, plus the additional revenue that he collected from the general commerce and trade within Israel, and from all the kings of Arabia, and the wealth gathered by his maritime expeditions to Ophir (India) and Tarshish (Spain). (II Chronicles 8:17-18, I Kings 10:22) All of this diverse material wealth flowed into Solomon's personal treasury.

One talent is about seventy-five pounds multiplied by six hundred sixty-six would equal approximately twenty-five tons of gold @ $1,250.00 per ounce would equal forty million dollars per ton, which would add up to be just beyond twenty-six billion sixty-four million dollars per year of personal income just in gold intake.

To go further with our reckoning, this sum multiplied by forty years would calculate to one trillion sixty-five billion six hundred million dollars.

This does not account for all the other honorariums, gifts, and overall general tax revenues that Solomon generated and/or collected from his various operations and all the other commercial trade activities by the citizens of Israel.

Applying today's standard investment rate of increase that generally says valuable assets will double every decade or so, we speculate that Solomon was safely in a class by himself with a multi-trillion-dollar personal net worth.

King David loved the Lord and desperately desired to build an appropriate house of rest for the ark of the covenant of his Maker. (I Chronicles17+22) However, the Lord did not allow King David to build His temple, but; God did give David the details to construct the temple and the operating plan for the divisions of the priests and the Levites, and for all the work of the service in the house of God. (I Chronicles 24-28)

Then with much difficulty and great personal sacrifice, King David focused his efforts to do everything he possibly could to accumulate the vast capital required, and to begin to gather and prepare the materials, and assemble the workforce necessary; (I Chronicles 29) to design, fabricate, and ultimately to build the exceedingly magnificent house to honor the presence of his Lord and his God.

In my affliction and trouble I have provided for the house of the Lord 100,000 talents of gold, 1,000,000 talents of silver, and bronze and iron without weighing. I have also provided timber and stone; you must add them. You have workmen in abundance: hewers, workers of stone and timber, and all kinds of craftsmen without number, skillful in doing every kind of work with gold, silver, bronze, and iron. So arise and be doing, and the Lord be with you!

David also commanded all the princes of Israel to help Solomon his son, saying, "Is not the Lord your God with you? And has He not given you peace on every side? For He has given the inhabitants of the land into my hand, and the land is subdued before the Lord and His people. Now set your mind and heart to seek (inquire of and require as your vital necessity) the Lord your God. Arise and build the sanctuary of the Lord God, so that the ark of the covenant of the Lord and the holy vessels of God may be brought into the house built to the Name and renown of the Lord.
I Chronicles 22:14-19 AMPC

The Tithe: 100,000 talents/gold +1,000,000 talents/silver

David's personal offering: 3,000 talents/gold + 7,000 talents/silver

Offering of the people: 5,002 talents/gold +10,000 talents/silver +18,000 talents /bronze + 100,000 talents/iron + unknown quantities of precious stones.

Gold 3,984 tons $159,360,000,000 + Silver 38,175 tons $38,175,000,000

Bronze 676 tons $3,200,000 + Iron 37,538 tons $10,000,000

Conservative estimated total value of the documented materials was one hundred ninety-seven billion five hundred thirty-five million dollars plus the other unknown quantities of quarried stone, cedar, and precious jewels.

Seven years labor for: 30,000 carpenters + 70,000 porters + 80,000 masons + 3,300 foremen = 183,300 men x 2000 man-hours per year x seven years = 2,566,200,000 man-hours @ $25.00 per hour = $64,155,000,000

Solomon commanded that all the work to prepare the building materials was to be completed off-site, in obedience to the Word. (Exodus 20:25, Deuteronomy 27:5)

Then Joshua built an altar to the Lord God of Israel on Mount Ebal, as Moses the servant of the Lord had commanded the children of Israel. As it is written in the Book of the Law of Moses, it was "an altar of uncut stones not shaped by iron tools." They sacrificed burnt offerings to the Lord on it, as well as peace offerings. Joshua 8:30-31 MEV

The house was built of stone prepared at the quarry, so that neither hammer nor axe nor any tool of iron was heard in the house while it was being built. I Kings 6:7 MEV

261.515 billion (x 1.7 minimum to capture the miscellaneous cost, plus inflation value over seven years) would equal $444,575,500,000 estimated cost of the Temple edifice, plus the value of the underlying forty +/- acres of real estate.

Wow, any four hundred forty-five billion-dollar construction project, that requires more than one hundred eighty-three thousand craftsmen, with a seven-year schedule of completion is a momentous achievement by anyone's standard, and certainly was in 966-959 BC.

So Solomon began to build the house of the Lord in Jerusalem on Mount Moriah, where He appeared to David his father, at the place that David established on the threshing floor of Ornan the Jebusite. He began to build in the second month on the second day during the fourth year of his reign. II Chronicles 3:1-2 MEV

Now the word of the Lord came to Solomon, saying, "Concerning this house which you are building, if you walk in My statutes and execute My judgements and keep all My commandments and walk in them, then I will carry out My word with you, which I spoke to David your father, and I will dwell among the people of Israel and will not forsake My people Israel." So Solomon built the house and finished it. I Kings 6:11-14 MEV

In the fourth year, in the month Ziv, the foundation of the house of the Lord was laid, and in the eleventh year, in the month Bul (which is the eight month), the house was completely finished. All the details and plans were met. So he took seven years to build it. I Kings 6:37-38 MEV

Solomon was beloved, blessed, and chosen by God to be the next king of Israel, and he was the favored son of King David and Bathsheba in his old age.

Prophetically named by God Almighty through his parents as Solomon (which means Peaceable); this child was also given the special name of Jedidiah (which means Beloved of Jehovah) by God Himself through the prophet Nathan. (II Samuel 12:24-25)

Solomon was selected by God to succeed his father David as sovereign monarch over His nation and His people, and to construct the Temple of the living God.

In addition to this impressive outline of blessings and favor, God Almighty made young Solomon the wisest, wealthiest, and the most extraordinarily intelligent man on the earth.

King Solomon was young, rich, powerful, handsome, popular, and very astute.

Solomon was the most affluent and brilliant statesman on the planet, and he had the presence of the Master and the Creator of the universe dwelling in the house he had built.

Notwithstanding all the blessings, favor, and God given wealth, glory, acumen, and honor; King Solomon had a very significant problem. Solomon was slipping further and further into apostasy, and accordingly; the last years of his life did not go well.

Oh my, those that have ears to hear, let them hear the Word of the Lord.

When you have come into the land which the Lord your God gives you and possess it and dwell there and say, "I will set a king over me just like all the nations that are around me," you must set a king over you whom the Lord your God will choose. You must select a king over you who is from among your brothers. You may not select a foreigner over you who is not your countryman. What is more, he shall not accumulate horses for himself or cause the people to return to Egypt in order that he accumulate horses, for the Lord has said to you, "You must not go back that way ever again." He shall not acquire many wives for himself, lest his heart turn away; nor shall he acquire for himself excess silver and gold. It must be, when he sits on the throne of his kingdom, that he shall write a copy of this law for himself on a scroll before the priests and the Levites. It must be with him, and he must read it all the days of his life so that he may learn to fear the Lord his God, and carefully observe all the words of this law and these statutes, and do them, that his heart will not be lifted up above his brothers and so that he may not turn aside from the commandment, to the right or to the left, to the end, so that he may prolong his days in his kingdom, he and his children, in the midst of Israel. Deuteronomy 17:14-20 MEV

Solomon began well and apparently, he did study and carefully heed the Word of God as commanded in the Scriptures and by his father David, because his life and activities reflected this awe and reverence for the Word and ways of God.

But then, in King Solomon's latter years; something drastically had changed.

Solomon acquired many foreign wives:

But Solomon loved many foreign women in addition to the daughter of Pharaoh, women of the Moabites, Ammonites, Edomites, Sidonians, and Hittites, from the nations which the Lord warned the children of Israel about, saying, "You shall not go in to them, nor shall they come in to you, for they will surely turn your heart away toward their gods." Solomon clung to these in love. He had seven hundred wives who were princesses and three hundred concubines, and his wives turned his heart away. For when Solomon was old, his wives turned his heart away after other gods, and his heart was not perfect with the Lord his God as the heart of David his father had been. I Kings 11:1-4 MEV

Even after his father David's previous warnings and God Almighty's very clear warning when God appeared to Solomon the second time, he betrayed God.

When Solomon had finished building the house of the Lord and the king's house and all else he desired, the Lord appeared to Solomon a second time, as He had appeared to him at Gibeon. The Lord said to him, I have heard your prayer and supplication, which you made before Me. I have consecrated this house which you built by putting My name there forever. And My eyes and My heart shall be there perpetually.

If you will walk before Me, as your father David walked, in integrity of heart and uprightness, so that you are obedient to do all that I have commanded you, and will keep My statutes and My judgements, then I will establish the throne of your kingdom upon Israel forever, just as I promised to your father David, saying, You shall not fail to have a man upon the throne of Israel.

But if you and your sons turn in any way from following Me and do not keep My commandments and My statues which I have set before you, but go and serve other gods and worship them, then I will cut Israel out of the land which I have given them, and I will cast this house, which I have consecrated for My name, out of My sight, and Israel shall be a proverb and a byword among all people. I Kings 9:1-7 MEV

Solomon broke covenant with God by pursuing his own personal desires and lusts and thus his heart become prideful. God Almighty not only said that He was going to take away his dominion, but; He was going to give it to one of Solomon's servants, after tearing it away from his son.

We all should prayerfully study to accurately discern the differences between David's heart of total devotion and Solomon's corrupted heart condition.

Therefore the Lord said to Solomon, Since you have done this and have not kept My covenant and statutes, which I commanded you, I will surely take the kingdom from you and give it to your servant. I will not do this in your lifetime for your father David's sake, but I will tear it out of the hand of your son. However, I will not take the whole kingdom away, but will preserve one tribe for your son for David My servant's sake and for the sake of Jerusalem which I chose. I Kings 11:11-13 MEV

Solomon acquired excessive measures of silver and gold:

The king made silver and gold in Jerusalem as abundant as stones and cedar as plentiful as sycamore trees in the lowlands of the Shephelah. II Chronicles 1:15 MEV

So King Solomon exceeded all the kings of the earth in terms of riches and wisdom. I Kings 10:23 MEV

Solomon accumulated many Egyptian horses:

This is God's way of saying to the Hebrews (and all of us) don't be faithless and do not build up large defenses because your God is the Lord of Hosts, and I AM your Provider and Protector.

Solomon gathered together chariots and horses. He had one thousand four hundred chariots and twelve thousand horses, and he put them in designated cities and with the king in Jerusalem. II Chronicles 1:14 MEV

The horses of Solomon were imported from Egypt and Kue, and the traders of the king would take them from Kue for a price. II Chronicles 1:16 MEV

Solomon's heart was lifted up, believing he deserved all the gold, all the glory, and all the girls:

Consequently, he mistreated his kinsmen through oppressive taxes to further increase his excessive wealth as he abused his power over God's children.

Your father made our yoke unbearable. Now, therefore, make the grievous service to your father and the heavy yoke he put upon us lighter, and we will serve you. I Kings 12:4 MEV

Solomon's apostasy resulted in the kingdom of Israel being forever divided. What a sad ending and the enduring legacy of the first prosperity preacher.

So, what do we do? What is the answer? Didn't God make Solomon rich? Yes, He did; but the more important question is why did God make him rich and wise and powerful?

Everyone who professes Jesus Christ as their Savior and their Lord have the very same promises that Father God made to Solomon, with the very same requirement: Total obedience and absolute submission to His Word, His will, and His ways.

King Jesus our Savior and Lord must have preeminence in all things in our hearts and lives, and then He shall provide all those things we need to completely fulfill everything Jesus has asked us to do for His Church during this age and train us for the Kingdom age to come. Trust Him. This is the Believer's mandate.

Now huge crowds were going along with [Jesus], and He turned and said to them, "I anyone comes to Me and does not hate his [own] father and mother [in the sense of indifference to or relative disregard for them in comparison with his attitude toward God] and [likewise] his wife and children and brothers and sisters – [yes] and even his own life also – he cannot be My disciple. Whoever does not persevere and carry his own cross and come after Me cannot be My disciple." Luke 14:25-27 AMPC

So then, any of you who does not forsake (renounce, surrender claim to, give up, say good-bye to) all that he has cannot be My disciple. Salt is good [an excellent thing], but if salt has lost its strength and has become saltless (insipid, flat), how shall its saltiness be restored? It is fit neither for the land nor for the manure heap; men throw it away. He who has ears to hear, let him listen and consider and comprehend by hearing! Luke 14:33-35 AMPC

Did Solomon lack anything whatsoever he needed to fulfill God's plan and purpose? No.

Why take thought about clothing? Consider the lilies of the field, how they grow: They neither work, nor do they spin. Yet I say to you that even Solomon in all his glory was not dressed like one of these. Therefore, if God so clothes the grass of the field, which today is here and tomorrow is thrown into the oven, will He not much more clothe you, O you of little faith? Therefore, take no thought, saying, 'What shall we eat?' or 'What shall we drink?' or 'What shall we wear?' (For the Gentiles seek after all these things.) For your heavenly Father knows that you have need of all these things. But seek first the kingdom of God and His righteousness, and all these things shall be given to you. Matthew 6:28-33 MEV

Do not be afraid, little flock, for it is your Father's good pleasure to give you the kingdom. Sell your possessions and give alms. Provide yourselves purses that do not grow old, an unfailing treasure in the heavens, where no thief comes near and no moth destroys. For where your treasure is, there will your heart be also. Luke 12:32-34 MEV

Did Solomon have God's supernatural supply? Yes.

God is able to make all grace abound toward you, so that you, always having enough of everything, may abound to every good work. II Corinthians 9:8 MEV

But my God shall supply your every need according to His riches in glory by Christ Jesus. Philippians 4:19 MEV

Did Solomon have great wisdom? Yes.

And I tell you, ask, and it will be given to you; seek, and you will find; knock, and it will be opened to you. For everyone who asks receives, and he who seeks finds, and to him who knocks it will be opened. If you then, being evil, know how to give good gifts to your children, how much more will your heavenly Father give the Holy Spirit to those who ask Him? Luke 11:9-10,13 MEV

If any of you lacks wisdom, let him ask of God, who gives to all men liberally and without criticism, and it will be given to him. James 1:5 MEV

Did Solomon dwell in peace? Yes.

Peace I leave with you. My peace I give to you. Not as the world gives do I give to you. Let not your heart be troubled, neither let it be afraid. John 14:27 MEV

Rejoice in the Lord always. Again I will say, rejoice! Let everyone come to know your gentleness. The Lord is at hand. Be anxious for nothing, but in everything, by prayer and supplication with gratitude, make your requests known to God. And the peace of God, which surpasses all understanding, will protect your hearts and minds through Christ Jesus. Philippians 4:4-7 MEV

For God has not given us the spirit of fear, but of power, and love, and self-control. II Timothy 1:7 MEV

Did Solomon build the temple and dwelling place of God? Yes.

Do you not know that you are the temple of God, and that the Spirit of God dwells in you? If anyone defiles the temple of God, God will destroy him. For the temple of God is holy. And you are His temple. I Corinthians 3:16-17 MEV

What? Do you not know that your body is the temple of the Holy Spirit, who is in you, whom you have received from God, and that you are not your own? You were bought with a price. Therefore glorify God in your body and in your spirit, which are God's. I Corinthians 6:19-20 MEV

But Christ is faithful over God's house as a Son, whose house we are if we hold fast the confidence and the rejoicing of our hope firm to the end. Hebrews 3:6 MEV

Was Solomon warned repeatedly not to worship other gods and Idols? Yes.

No servant can serve two masters. Either he will hate the one and love the other, or he will be loyal to one and despise the other. You cannot serve God and wealth. Luke 16:13 MEV

Did Solomon get discontented, even with all his riches and pleasure? Yes.

But godliness with contentment is great gain. For we brought nothing into this world, and it is certain that we can carry nothing out. If we have food and clothing, we shall be content with these things. But those who desire to be rich fall into temptation and a snare and into many foolish and harmful lusts, which drown men in ruin and destruction. For the love of money is the root of all evil. While coveting after money, some have strayed from the faith and pierced themselves through with many sorrows. I Timothy 6:6-10 MEV

Did Solomon lose the awe of God, forsake his first love, and thus lead Israel into sin? Yes.

At that time the disciples came up and asked Jesus, Who then is [really] the greatest in the kingdom of heaven? And He called a little child to Himself and put

him in the midst of them, and said, Truly I say to you, unless you repent (change, turn about) and become like little children [trusting, lowly, loving, forgiving], you can never enter the kingdom of heaven [at all]. Whoever will humble himself therefore and become like this little child [trusting, lowly, loving, forgiving] is the greatest in the kingdom of heaven. And whoever receives and accepts and welcomes one little child like this for My sake and in My name receives and accepts and welcomes Me. But whoever causes one of these little ones who believe in and acknowledge and cleave to Me to stumble and sin [that is, who entices him or hinders him in right conduct or thought], it would be better (more expedient and profitable or advantageous) for him to have a great millstone fastened around his neck and to be sunk in the depth of the sea.
Matthew 18:1-6 AMPC

But I have this [one charge to make] against you: that you have left (abandoned) the love that you had at first [you have deserted Me, your first love]. Remember then from what heights you have fallen. Repent (change the inner man to meet God's will) and do the works you did previously [when first you knew the Lord], or else I will visit you and remove your lampstand from its place, unless you change your mind and repent. Revelation 2:4-5 AMPC

Each one of us must always be in remembrance of why Father God has given His people the ability to create wealth here in the earth. It is clearly outlined for us in Deuteronomy chapter eight what will be our end if we do not obey His Word.

When you have eaten and are full, then you shall bless the Lord your God for the good land which He has given you. Beware that you do not forget the Lord your God by not keeping His commandments, and His judgements, and His statutes, which I am commanding you today. Otherwise, when you have eaten and are full and have built and occupied good houses, and when your herds and your flocks multiply, and all that you have multiplies, then your heart will become proud and you will forget the Lord your God who brought you out of the land of Egypt, from the house of slavery, who led you through that great and terrible wilderness, where there were fiery serpents and scorpions and drought, where there was on water, who brought forth for you water out of the rock of flint, who fed you in the wilderness with manna, which your fathers did not know, that He might humble you and that He might prove you, to do good for you in the end. Otherwise, you may say in your heart, "My power and the might of my hand have gained me this wealth." But you must remember the Lord your God, for it is He who gives you the ability to get wealth, so that He may establish His covenant which He swore to your fathers, as it is today. If you ever forget the Lord your God and go after other gods and serve them and worship them, then I testify against you today that you will surely perish. Just like the nations which the Lord will destroy before you, so shall you perish because you would not be obedient to the voice of the Lord your God. Deuteronomy 8:10-19 MEV

This is exactly what King Solomon did. He forgot the Lord! Solomon obviously did not continue to study the Word of God and heed the commandments therein. Solomon was commanded to be in the Word every day, just like we are.

Subsequently he initiated the honor and worship of the Idol gods of all his foreign wives and his heart was lifted up with pride. Solomon began to think and believe, with much encouragement (no doubt) from his many wives, that he had somehow managed to create and multiply all this incredible wealth, power, and magnificence that the Lord had given to him to steward.

Solomon, at some point; must have begun to truly believe that it was because of his great mind and acumen that he was so rich, powerful, and influential; and that he really did earn and thus deserve all the gold, all the glory, and all the girls.

Command those who are rich in this world that they not be conceited, nor trust in uncertain riches, but in the living God, who richly gives us all things to enjoy. Command that they do good, that they be rich in good works, generous, willing to share, and laying up in store for themselves a good foundation for the coming age, so that they may take hold of eternal life. I Timothy 6:17-19 MEV

This supposed "prosperity message" is consistent throughout the Scriptures.

Jesus Christ is Lord of everything. He is the one who gives us the ability to create wealth and that every single thing in heaven and earth is all His. All the riches of the world are owned by our King, and He directs them has He alone sees fit to assign these resources for the completion of His master plan of redemption and restoration of His creation. Amen.

The silver is Mine, and the gold is Mine, says the Lord of Hosts. Haggai 2:8 MEV

He is the image of the invisible God and the firstborn of every creature. For by Him all things were created that are in heaven and that are in earth, visible and invisible, whether they are thrones, or dominions, or principalities, or powers. All things were created by Him and for Him. He is before all things, and in Him all things hold together. He is the head of the body, the church. He is the beginning, the firstborn from the dead, so that in all things He may have the preeminence. For it pleased the Father that in Him all fullness should dwell, and to reconcile all things to Himself by Him, having made peace through the blood of His cross, by Him, I say – whether they are things in earth, or things in heaven. Colossians 1:15-20 MEV

Our Lord Jesus shall provide for us absolutely everything that we need to accomplish His plans and purposes that He has ordained for us to complete, and we must have faith that He will do just that. Jesus did not promise to give us all the wealth we want to fulfill our plans.

Then Jesus called together the Twelve [apostles] and gave them power and authority over all demons, and to cure diseases, and He sent them out to announce and preach the kingdom of God and to bring healing. And He said to them, Do not take anything for your journey – neither walking stick, nor wallet [for a collection bag], nor food of any kind, nor money, and do not have two undergarments (tunics). And whatever house you enter, stay there until you go away [from that place]. And wherever they do not receive and accept and welcome you, when you leave that town shake off [even] the dust from your feet, as testimony against them. And departing, they went about from village to village, preaching the Gospel and restoring the afflicted to health everywhere. Luke 9:1-6 AMPC

Now after this the Lord chose and appointed seventy others and sent them out ahead of Him, two by two, into every town and place where He Himself was about to come (visit). And He said to them, The harvest indeed is abundant [there is much ripe grain], but the farmhands are few. Pray therefore the Lord of the harvest to send out laborers into His harvest. Go your way; behold, I send you out like lambs into the midst of wolves. Carry no purse, no provisions bag, no [change of] sandals; refrain from [retarding your journey by] saluting and wishing anyone well along the way. Whatever house you enter, first say, Peace be to this household! [Freedom from all the distresses that result from sin be with this family]. And if anyone [worthy] of peace and blessedness is there, the peace and blessedness you wish shall come upon him; but if not, it shall come back to you. And stay on in the same house, eating and drinking what they provide, for the laborer is worthy of his wages. Do not keep moving from house to house. Whenever you go into a town and they receive and accept and welcome you, eat what is set before you; and heal the sick in it and say to them, The kingdom of God has come to you. Luke 10:1-9 AMPC

And He said to them, When I sent you out with no purse or [provision] bag or sandals, did you lack anything? They answered, Nothing! Luke 22:35 AMPC

What did they lack? Nothing!

Our great God and Savior has given us everything that we have in our possession for us to steward on His behalf, and we shall never lack any good thing that we need to completely and totally fulfill the calling that He has designed for our lives. If God guides, He provides; but we must submit to His Lordship and have faith in His Word.

No Lack! for His servants – this is the true prosperity message of our Lord and King Jesus.

King David, the man after God's own heart; had experienced many ups and downs in his life as he learned to deny his flesh, and die to his soul, and thus fully follow the Lord. David truly understood the Scriptural prosperity message, as evidenced by his final recorded prayer to his Lord that he dearly loved, believed, and faithfully followed through his obedience.

Therefore David blessed the Lord before all the assembly and said,

Be praised, adored, and thanked, O Lord, the God of Israel our [forefather], forever and ever. Yours, O Lord, is the greatness and the power and the glory and the victory and the majesty, for all that is in the heavens and the earth is Yours; Yours is the kingdom, O Lord, and Yours it is to be exalted as Head over all. Both riches and honor come from You, and You reign over all. In Your hands are power and might; in Your hands it is to make great and to give strength to all.

Now therefore, our God, we thank you and praise Your glorious name and those attributes which that name denotes. But who am I, and what are my people, that we should retain strength and be able to offer thus so willingly? For all things come from You, and out of Your own [hand] we have given You. For we are strangers before You, and sojourners, as all our fathers were; our days on the earth are like a shadow, and there is no hope or expectation of remaining.

O Lord our God, all this store that we have prepared to build You a house for Your holy Name and the token of Your presence comes from Your hand, and is all Your own.

I know also, my God, that You try the heart and delight in uprightness. In the uprightness of my heart I have freely offered all these things. And now I have seen with joy Your people who are present here offer voluntarily and freely to You.

O Lord, God of Abraham, Isaac, and Israel, our fathers, keep forever such purposes and thoughts in the minds of Your people, and direct and establish their hearts toward You.

And give to Solomon my son a blameless heart to keep Your commandments, testimonies, and statutes, and to do all that is necessary to build the palace [for You] for which I have made provision.

And David said to all the assembly, "Now adore (praise and thank) the Lord your God!" And all the assembly blessed the Lord, the God of their fathers, and bowed down and did obeisance to the Lord and to the king [as His earthly representative]. Amen. I Chronicles 29:10-20 AMPC

We believe that King Solomon got the Truth sorted out in his heart and mind and repented before his passing from this life. Why would we make such a statement?

Because here following are the last recorded words of wisdom, from the last verses, from the last chapter, of the last book that the prosperity preacher uttered at the end of his natural life. Here is King Solomon's inspired summation:

And in addition to being wise, the Preacher still taught the people knowledge, and he considered, sought out, and arranged many proverbs. And the Preacher sought to discover words of delight, and to write in uprightness words of truth. The words of the wise are like goads, and the collected sayings are like firmly embedded nails, given by one shepherd. My son, beware of anything beyond these. Of making many books there is no end, and much study is a weariness to the flesh. Now, all had been heard. Let us hear the conclusion of the matter:

Fear God and keep His commandments, for this is the whole duty of man. For God will bring every deed into judgement, including every secret thing, whether good or evil. Ecclesiastes 12:9-14 MEV

No Lack. This is the prosperity message of our Lord and soon coming King, and we are all expected to follow however to wherever the Holy Spirit would lead us in complete faith that all our needs will be fully supplied by our Lord.

This is the Believer's mandate.

CHAPTER ELEVEN

Go, make disciples

Foundational Truth: Jesus came to save every tribe, tongue, people, and nation on the earth, and all believers have been commanded to first become a disciple themselves, and then to go and make more disciples of Jesus Christ.

Father God desires that all mankind would come to salvation. (John 3:16-17, II Timothy 2:1-7) And the primary way God commands us to accomplish this task is through preaching and teaching of the good news of Jesus Christ to all humanity, and thus all believers are fully commissioned to go and do this beginning with our own homes and families, and then reaching our friends with the good news, and then beyond; wherever the Lord would lead us to go.

Go, Make Disciples

We all know about this Great Commission, don't we? At the very least, we all have heard about it, right? Well, no we all do not know nor have we all heard. Matter of fact, according to the findings of new research completed and published (March of 2018) by the folks at *Barna Group*, that when U.S. Church attenders were asked if they had heard of the Great Commission; here is a summary of the churchgoers responses: 51% answered *No*, and 25% answered *Yes, but could not recall the exact meaning*, and another 6% answered *I'm not sure*. Wow, more than eight out of ten of those surveyed that are professing Christians and attend Church have not heard of the Great Commission, or if they have at least heard the terminology, they are not clear what exactly it means.

This is an incredibly sad report for the Church. Our human tendencies are to begin to think about all the reasons why these numbers are so poor, but; the bottom line is the body of Christ "the Church" is not fulfilling one of its primary objectives of existence. Is it any wonder why the Church is not making true disciples and followers of Jesus Christ? So, what shall we do? We must go back to the basics and review the fundamentals of our faith and our calling.

The Believer's Mandate

We shall begin this foundational Truth with the Scriptures that define the Great Commission because this phrase the Great Commission is not in the Bible, so; let's make certain we know exactly why it is called a "commission" and what is so "great" about it. Here following are the last recorded words, prayers, commands and commissions of our Lord & Savior, Jesus Christ; before His ascension back to the right hand of the Father in heaven.

Jesus approached and, breaking the silence, said to them, All authority (all power of rule) in heaven and on earth has been given to Me. Go then and make disciples of all the nations, baptizing them into the name of the Father and of the Son and of the Holy Spirit, teaching them to observe everything that I have commanded you, and behold, I am with you all the days (perpetually, uniformly, and on every occasion), to the [very] close and consummation of the age. Amen (so let it be). Matthew 28:18-20 AMPC

Afterward He appeared to the Eleven [apostles themselves] as they reclined at table; and He reproved and reproached them for their unbelief (their lack of faith) and their hardness of heart, because they had refused to believe those who had seen Him and looked at Him attentively after He had risen [from death].

Go, Make Disciples

And He said to them, Go into all the world and preach and publish openly the good news (the Gospel) to every creature [of the whole human race]. He who believes [who adheres to and trusts in and relies on the Gospel and Him Whom it sets forth] and is baptized will be saved [from the penalty of eternal death]; but he who does not believe [who does not adhere to and trust in and rely on the Gospel and Him Whom it sets forth] will be condemned. And these attesting signs will accompany those who believe: in My name they will drive demons; they will speak in new languages; they will pick up serpents; and [even] if they drink anything deadly, it will not hurt them; they will lay their hands on the sick, and they will get well. So then the Lord Jesus, after He had spoken to them, was taken up into heaven and He sat down at the right hand of God. And they went out and preached everywhere, while the Lord kept working with them and confirming the message by the attesting signs and miracles that closely accompanied [it]. Amen (so be it). Mark 16:14-20 AMPC

Then He said to them, This is what I told you while I was still with you: everything which is written concerning Me in the Law of Moses and the Prophets and the Psalms must be fulfilled. Then He [thoroughly]

opened up their minds to understand the Scriptures, and said to them, Thus it is written that the Christ (the Messiah) should suffer and on the third day rise from (among) the dead, and that repentance [with a view to and as the condition of] forgiveness of sins should be preached in His name to all nations, beginning from Jerusalem. You are witnesses of these things. And behold, I will send forth upon you what My Father has promised; but remain in the city [Jerusalem] until you are clothed with power from on high. Then He conducted them out as far as Bethany, and, lifting up His hands, He invoked a blessing on them. And it occurred that while He was blessing them, He parted from them and was taken up into heaven.

Luke 24:44-51 AMPC

Just as You sent Me into the world, I also have sent them into the world. And so for their sake and on their behalf I sanctify (dedicate, consecrate) Myself, that they also may be sanctified (dedicated, consecrated, made holy) in the Truth. Neither for these alone do I pray [it is not for their sake only that I make this request], but also for all those who will ever come to believe in (trust in, cling to, rely on) Me through their word and teaching, that they all may be one, [just] as You, Father, are in Me and I in You, that they also may be one in Us, so that the world may believe and be convinced that You have sent Me. John 17:18-21 AMPC

Then Jesus said to them again, Peace to you! [Just] as the Father has sent Me forth, so I am sending you. And having said this, He breathed on them and said to them, Receive the Holy Spirit! John 20:21-22 AMPC

And while being in their company and eating with them, He commanded them not to leave Jerusalem but to wait for what the Father had promised, Of which [He said] you have heard Me speak. For John baptized with water, but not many days from now you shall be baptized with (placed in, introduced into) the Holy Spirit. But you shall receive power (ability, efficiency, and might) when the Holy Spirit has come upon you, and you shall be My witnesses in Jerusalem and all Judea and Samaria and the ends (the very bounds) of the earth. Acts 1:4-5,8 AMPC

A synopsis of all these Scriptures could be simply stated that we believers are called to become disciples of Jesus, and we are to go and teach others to be disciples of Jesus too.... this is the Believer's Mandate.

No one knows for sure when or who was the first to articulate the expression "the Great Commission", but; a Christian missionary from Britain to China for over fifty years by the name of Hudson Taylor (1832-1905)

is the man credited for popularizing the maxim, the great commission; as a summarized description of his activities as he went about his evangelistic work of making thousands of disciples for Christ among the Chinese people, and encouraging them all to go and do likewise.

This foundational Truth that all nations, tribes, peoples, and tongues are called to become disciples of Jesus Christ is one Truth that most professing Christians would absolutely agree upon, however; only a few could actually explain to you what a real disciple is or how to become one, and even fewer could honestly say that they themselves were a true disciple of Jesus Christ.

This should not be so, however; this is the reality in much of the Church today. We shall begin with a brief description of the discipleship program and the original course work that was commonly practiced throughout Israel during the days of Jesus growing up in Galilee, subsequently; we should all have a greater level of understanding of what Jesus meant to communicate to us when He commanded all believers to first become a disciple ourselves, and then commissioned us to go and make disciples of all peoples and all nations.

Jesus would have been referring to this very same discipleship program that was widely known and would have been common knowledge to His followers and to any audience He would encounter throughout the middle eastern region.

In the first century AD, the Rabbinical educational procedure book in Israel was called *Mishnah*, which means study by repetition or "to study and review", and the first textbook was the Torah, or the first five books of the Hebrew Scriptures, and the first classroom was the local place of worship or the community Synagogue.

A child growing up during the first century AD and living anywhere in Israel would have been expected to attend daily studies at the local Synagogue. The community would have employed an instructor for the school and would have respectfully called him Rabbi to recognize his position as a teacher of the Scriptures, but; he would not carry any special authority (not ordained by the Great Sanhedrin) at the Synagogue.

The Primary School or *Beit Sefer* (House of the Book). This elementary training began for boys and girls at age five until ten years of age, and the focus was reading, writing, and memorizing Scripture. The goal was for each student to know and quote the entire

Torah from memory. Beyond this point in schooling all the girls and most of the boys would stay at home and learn the family trade, vocation, or business. It would be after this time that a young man would be allowed to attend his first Passover feast in Jerusalem.

The Secondary School or *Beit Talmud* (House of Learning). This stage of teaching would continue for the very best students among the boys only from 10 until 15 years of age. They would continue their study and memorization of the Prophets and the Writings (the Hebrew Scriptures) in addition to the Torah. The very best among the top students could quote from memory the complete Torah, Prophets and the Writings. (the entire Old Testament) These young men would also be expected to continue to learn the family vocation or business in addition to their continued study of the Scriptures.

We know Jesus went to His first Passover in Jerusalem when He was twelve years of age (Luke 2:40-42), and that He increased in wisdom and in stature and years, and in favor with God and man (Luke 2:52), suggesting that He continued to study the Scriptures and the Talmud (Oral Law), and pursuing the family vocation as a Carpenter (Mark 6:3) and we also know from Scripture that Jesus began His public ministry at the age of thirty. (Luke 3:23)

The High School or *Beit Midrash* (House of Study). The brightest and the very best students among the truly exceptional scholars sought permission to leave their home, family, friends, vocation, and village to go and continue their studies with one of Israel's top Rabbi with authority (ordained by the Great Sanhedrin). Most of these superior students would seek out the specific Rabbi (Master Teacher) they desired to "follow" because they would be pledging to go and live and travel with the Rabbi for an extended period, in most cases more than a decade of years. Once the student had permission and the blessing of his family, he would then approach the Rabbi he had chosen and request to be his disciple. If the Rabbi accepted the potential students petition, he would be allowed to follow the Master and "take his yoke" and be received as a disciple. The proper name for this student in Hebrew would be called *Talmid* (disciple) or *Talmidim* (disciples). We must understand that a disciple is not the normal university student as we think of one who is going to some institution of higher learning today. A typical academic student as we would normally see today is attending classes and completing the necessary course work to acquire what they need to know to pass a series of examinations, earning a grade, with the goal of eventually graduating with some sort of a degree.

To distinguish this typical educational scenario to the Rabbi and the disciples relationship is quite a different scenario indeed. The disciple is completely devoted to their Rabbi. The college student is looking to pass a test or complete a course, but in contrast; the disciple wants to literally become one with his Rabbi. This relationship between the disciple and Rabbi is very rigorous with the disciple absorbing every thought, word, and deed. The disciple intends to so closely observe and follow his Master as to ultimately duplicate his Rabbi (Teacher) in every way. The stated goal of every Talmid was to in due course become his Rabbi, and this was clearly understood by all Master Teachers and all potential disciples.

The name Rabbi isn't really a job title or occupation, it is more of an expression and an acknowledgement of the Master out of respect and honor for that individual because of their great authority. The Torah teachers, which were usually referred to as lawyers and scribes; could only teach accepted and established Rabbinical interpretations. The Master-Rabbi-Teacher with authority (ordained by the Great Sanhedrin) could make new or amended interpretations and could establish binding legal judgements and rulings in accordance with the Scriptures.

When Jesus finished these sayings, the people were astonished at His teaching, for He taught them as one having authority, and not as the scribes. Matthew 7:28-29 MEV

They went to Capernaum, and immediately on the Sabbath He entered the synagogue and taught. They were astonished at His teaching, for He taught them as one having authority, and not as the scribes. Mark 1:21-22 MEV

The lawyers called Jesus Master-Rabbi-Teacher (depending on your English translation of the Bible) in Luke 11:45 and the blind beggar named Bartimaeus called Jesus Rabbi in Mark 10:51 and ordinary citizens called Jesus Master in Luke 12:13 and Pharisees called Jesus Master in Luke 19:39 and Sadducees called Jesus Master in Luke 20:28 and scribes called Jesus Master in Luke 20:39 and the Rich Young Ruler called Jesus Master in Luke 18:18 and the disciples called Jesus Master in John 1:38 and Nicodemus called Jesus Master in John 3:2 and the people of Tiberias called Jesus Master in John 6:25 and Jesus called

Himself Master in John 13:13 and Mary Magdalene called Jesus Rabboni in John 20:16 and even the chief priests, scribes and the elders representing the Great Sanhedrin recognized that Jesus spoke, taught, and operated in great authority in Mark 11:27-28, even if they had not granted this authority to Him.

The decision to approach, petition, and ultimately pledge devotion to the Rabbi that the student had chosen, (assuming, of course, that the Rabbi granted the students request to become his *Talmid* or disciple), was an extraordinary commitment. It meant absolute total submission of the disciples will to the Master's requirements. This obligation meant the disciple would literally surrender and yield all his thoughts, opinions, plans, dreams, desires, goals, and aspirations to follow and faithfully serve his chosen Master. It meant that you were totally committed to be the bond-servant to your Master until you became transformed into the image and likeness of your Rabbi in thought, word, and deed.

The clear majority of these exceptional students would seek out the Rabbi they wanted to follow and find favor with, however; the truly rare and exceptional Rabbi would choose his own Talmidim. It was very, very unusual for any Rabbi to seek out and come to his potential students with the invitation to "follow me" because the ultimate goal is for the disciple to become just like his Master Teacher. Therefore, this Rabbi would need to possess tremendous supernatural confidence in the chosen student's ability to become transformed into his image in thought, word and deed and thus become just like him in every way.

Or this extraordinary Rabbi would have to be the Son of the living God.

You did not choose Me, but I chose you, and appointed you, that you should go and bear fruit, and that your fruit should remain, that the Father may give you whatever you ask of Him in My name. John 15:16 MEV

You and I have been sough-out and called by the Master to come and follow Him, and to become His disciples, but; what will you chose? You now know how Jesus defines a disciple and what He expects of all His true devoted followers. This is our clarion call, and this is exactly why we are here.

This is the Believer's Mandate.

Chapter twelve

Do what He did

Foundational Truth: If we do what Jesus did, then we will do what Jesus did.

Up to this point, we have been laying a Truth foundation that teaches us we are all called to become transformed into the image of Jesus Christ and we are commanded to imitate Jesus in every way. This is the Believer's Mandate.

In this chapter, we shall establish more specifically what Jesus did during His three and a half years of earthy ministry that we are commissioned to be copying and duplicating here and now all around the globe as individual members of His body.

The very last night that Jesus was with His disciples, He shared some awesome Truths about the future and what would be the expectation of everyone that chooses to believe and obey Jesus and becomes His disciple, and thus walk as He walked.

Truly, truly I say to you, he who believes in Me will do the works that I do also. And he will do greater works than these, because I am going to My Father. I will do whatever you ask in My name, that the Father may be glorified in the Son. If you ask anything in My name, I will do it. John 14:12-14 MEV

If you remain in Me, and My words remain in you, you will ask whatever you desire, and it shall be done for you. My Father is glorified by this, that you bear much fruit; so you will be My disciples. John 15:7-8 MEV

Whoever says he abides in Him ought [as a personal debt] to walk and conduct himself in the same way in which He walked and conducted Himself. I John 2:6 AMPC

It is very clear in the Scriptures that Jesus has commanded every believer to become disciples ourselves, which means to follow in His footsteps in every way, and to go forth, imitating Jesus and doing all the works Jesus had been doing. We are also to make disciples of everyone that would choose to believe Jesus and to teach them to do the same thing, thus the body of Christ would grow and expand and fill the earth with the good news that Jesus is alive, and that Jesus saves, and Jesus heals, and Jesus delivers today, just as He always has. Do you believe this?

Let us go back to the Scriptures and see exactly what was prophesied about Jesus before He came in the flesh as the Son of Man. Of course, you can find Jesus in every book of the Bible through types, shadows, similitudes and patterns. We also know that there were more than three hundred prophecies spoken and recorded in the Scriptures hundreds of years before Jesus came in the flesh. These three hundred prophecies were just about Jesus' birth, life, death, and resurrection; and each one was perfectly fulfilled. This is how you prove the reliability of the Word of God is through fulfilled prophecies and thus everything that God has said shall come to pass. We will highlight a few here for our study of what was foretold about Jesus and compare those prophetic words to His life and His earthly ministry.

The Spirit of the Lord God is upon me because the Lord has anointed me to preach good news to the poor; He has sent me to heal the broken-hearted, to proclaim liberty to the captives, and the opening of the prison to those who are bound; to proclaim the acceptable year of the Lord….. Isaiah 61:1-2a MEV

This was prophesied about the mission of the Jewish Messiah more than seven hundred years before Jesus was born in Bethlehem, and then was publicly declared fulfilled by Jesus Himself in the synagogue at Nazareth approximately one year after Jesus' earthy ministry had begun.

He came to Nazareth, where He had been brought up. And as His custom was, He went to the synagogue on the Sabbath day. And He stood to read. The scroll of the prophet Isaiah was handed to Him. When He had unrolled the scroll, He found the place where it was written: The Spirit of the Lord is upon Me, because He has anointed Me to preach the gospel to the poor; He has sent Me to heal the broken-hearted, to preach deliverance to the captives and recovery of sight to the blind, to set at liberty those who are oppressed; to preach the acceptable year of the Lord. Then He rolled up the scroll, and gave it back to the attendant, and sat down. The eyes of all those who were in the synagogue were fixed on Him. And He began to say to them, Today this Scripture is fulfilled in your hearing. Luke 4:16-21 MEV

When the original scrolls of the various books of the Bible were written down, the text was not separated by chapter (added in the 12th century AD) and verse (added in the 16th century AD), and the reason Jesus stopped reading midway through verse two of Isaiah sixty-one that day in Nazareth is because that was the limit of what had been fulfilled thus far by Jesus Christ. The balance of Isaiah 61:2b ....*and the day of vengeance of our God;* is prophesying about Jesus' second coming, which has not occurred yet, and hence has not been fulfilled, but; it most certainly will be one day very soon. The day of vengeance of our God is the second coming of Jesus to earth on judgement day. It shall be the day of reckoning for all the nations and those remaining inhabitants of the earth. This will not be a good day for all those that did not choose to accept Jesus as their Savior and Lord. (see Revelation 19:11-21)

The Spirit of the Lord is upon Me, because He has anointed Me..... Luke 4:18a MEV

The Holy Spirit came upon Jesus because Father God had anointed Jesus with the Holy Spirit, which is the promise of the Father. We see recorded in the gospels that on Jesus' thirtieth birthday (Luke 3:23) He came to the river Jordon to be baptized by John the Baptizer, who was the forerunner prophesied in Isaiah 40:3-5 and in Malachi 3:1, to go before Jesus the Christ, and when Jesus came up out of the water, the Holy Spirit came upon Him, thus anointing Him for His earthly ministry. (Matthew 3:1-17, Mark 1:1-11, Luke 3:1-22, John 1:19-34) Before this day when the Holy Spirit came upon Jesus, He had not performed one single miracle. The day Father God sent the Holy Spirit to anoint Jesus with power marks the day that Jesus' earthy ministry officially began.

Jesus was and is the prophesied Messiah, (which comes from the Hebrew word Mashiach) which means Anointed One (Psalm 2:2, John 1:41, Acts 2:36), and when we say the English word Christ, which came from the Greek word Christos, we are saying the very same thing. The Hebrew word "Mashiach" equals Messiah in English and the Greek word "Christos" equals Christ in English, and all these Hebrew, Greek, and English words all mean Anointed One. So, when we say Jesus Christ, we are saying Jesus the Anointed One, and the anointing is the gift of the Father, the mighty Holy Spirit.

Jesus went throughout all Galilee teaching in their synagogues, preaching the gospel of the kingdom, and healing all kinds of sickness and all sorts of diseases among the people. His fame went throughout all Syria. And they brought to Him all sick people who were taken with various diseases and tormented with

The Believer's Mandate

pain, those who were possessed with demons, those who had seizures, and those who had paralysis, and He healed them. Matthew 4:23-25 MEV

How God anointed and consecrated Jesus of Nazareth with the [Holy] Spirit and with strength and ability and power; how He went about doing good and, in particular, curing all who were harassed and oppressed by [the power of] the devil, for God was with Him. Acts 10:38 AMPC

So, did Jesus the Christ (the Anointed One) go about preaching the gospel, teaching the word, and healing the blind, sick, deaf, and the lame? Did Jesus cast out demons, cleanse the lepers, and raise the dead? Did Jesus calm the storms, walk on water, multiply bread and fish, and turn water into wine? Did Jesus restore the oppressed, discouraged, and the broken hearted? Yes, He most certainly did! And Jesus Christ is alive today, and He is still doing all those awesome things through His anointed body on earth, which is the Church; even today.

The foundational Truth in this chapter is: If we do what Jesus did, then we will do what Jesus did. So, what exactly did Jesus do to walk in this power, anointing, and authority? Jesus became 30-fold soil, and then 60-fold soil, and ultimately 100-fold soil, as

He taught us in the *Parable of the Sower*, and we must do the very same thing. So, what exactly does this mean, and what does it look like?

Remember, we are spirit beings, and we have a soul, and we live in our bodies. Jesus came as the Son of Man in the flesh to be our ultimate example, so Jesus had to learn to die to His fleshly desires, just as we must also die to our fleshly desires to mature into 30-fold fruitful soil.

In the days of His flesh, Jesus offered up prayers and supplications with loud cries and tears to Him who was able to save Him from death. He was heard because of His godly fear. Though He was a Son, He learned obedience through the things that He suffered, Hebrews 5:7-8 MEV

Once the born-again believer begins his or her new life in Christ, the first thing we must deal with is our fleshly lusts and desires, and again, Jesus is our example here, every time, and in every way, and before Jesus began His earthly ministry, He did something and received something of great importance.

We see in the Scriptures outlined above, that Jesus went to John the Baptist at the river Jordon to be baptized and when He came up out of the water, the heavens opened, and the Holy Spirit came upon Him, and Father God spoke from heaven: And a voice came from heaven, saying, This is My beloved Son, in whom I am well pleased. Matthew 3:17 MEV

The reason that Father God spoke these awesome words from heaven as a witness was because in the middle eastern culture during the preceding centuries, a man could have many male offspring, but; none of them were a son until the father declared him a son.

To explain this fact another way, the patriarch could choose the son or sons from his male offspring in which to pass along his wealth and his authority into the future. When the first century father declared a son, of which he was well pleased, meant that the son now could conduct family business and would have been considered an equal to the father in power to act with all legal binding authority. This head of the family or tribal Chief would then expect all others to treat his chosen heir with the same respect that they would give to the father in all matters. Many times, the patriarch would select and adopt a son in which to pass along the family heritage.

There were often many reasons for this, but; the most obvious would have been in the occurrence that the father did not have a natural born son living in which to transfer all his affluence, assets, and authority.

However, even if the firstborn son was alive and well pleasing to the father, the adopted son would consistently receive a double portion inheritance and would be considered at the very lease a co-heir with the firstborn natural son. The adopted, or chosen son, was permanently and significantly honored in the eastern cultures, and would have been considered the highest-ranking royal heir to the patriarch.

Father God was declaring to all that Jesus was His Beloved Son, and that He was well pleased with Him and that Father God had just bestowed upon Jesus all power and all authority to conduct family business on earth as the Son of Man and as the Son of God, therefore we should listen, honor, and obey Jesus' words.

In case anyone had forgotten, at approximately the midpoint of Jesus' three and a half-year earthy ministry, at the event known as the Mount of Transfiguration recorded in Matthew chapter 17, Mark chapter 9, and Luke chapter 9, we see Father God reminding us of exactly who Jesus is. This event was witnessed by Peter, John, and James.

Then there came a voice out of the cloud, saying, This is My Son, My Chosen One or My Beloved; listen to and yield to and obey Him! Luke 9:35 AMPC

And as an eyewitness, Peter records this event in his epistle to the church also.

For we were not following cleverly devised stories when we made known to you the power and the coming of our Lord Jesus Christ (the Messiah), but we were eyewitnesses of His majesty (grandeur, authority of sovereign power). For when He was invested with honor and glory from God the Father and a voice was borne to Him by the [splendid] Majestic Glory [in the bright cloud that overshadowed Him, saying], This is My beloved Son in Whom I am well pleased and delight, we [actually] heard this voice borne out of heaven, for we were together with Him on the holy mountain. II Peter 1:16-18 AMPC

Okay, let's go back to the river Jordan and see what was the very first thing that Jesus, the Beloved and Chosen Son of God did after He became the Christ, the Anointed One. We shall find the details recorded in the Gospels of Matthew 4:1-11, Mark 1:12-13, and Luke 4:1-13.

Jesus, being filled with the Holy Spirit, returned from the Jordan and was led by the Spirit into the wilderness, being tempted by the devil for forty days. During those days He ate nothing. And when they were ended, He was hungry. Luke 4:1-2 MEV

The very first event of Jesus' ministry after He was anointed by the Holy Spirit, was to willingly submit to the leading of the Holy Spirit, and to go directly into the wilderness with no provision whatsoever, to be tempted and tried by the devil.

Jesus had to deny Himself and die to His fleshly desires, just as we must. There is much to be said about these Scriptures and there are many very important lessons here for us to glean from this event in the life of Jesus, but; we shall endeavor to highlight some of them here for our study of what Jesus did, so; that we shall know what we are supposed to do in order to fully imitate Him.

Temptation number one – Lust of the flesh

The devil said to Him, If you are the Son of God, command this stone to become bread. Luke 4:3 MEV

Jesus answered him, It is written, Man shall not live by bread alone, but by every word of God. Luke 4:4 MEV

How Jesus overcame the test: He quoted the Word from Deuteronomy 8:3

Temptation number two – Lust of the eyes

The devil, taking Him up onto a high mountain, showed Him all the kingdoms of the world in a moment of time. And the devil said to Him, I will give You all this power and their glory, for it has been delivered to me. And I give it to whomever I will. If You, then, will worship me, all will be Yours. Luke 4:5-7 MEV

And Jesus answered him, Get behind Me, Satan! For it is written, You shall worship the Lord your God, and Him only shall you serve. Luke 4:8 MEV

How Jesus overcame the test: He quoted the Word from Deuteronomy 6:13

Temptation number three – Pride of life

He brought Him to Jerusalem, set Him on the pinnacle of the temple, and said to Him, If You are the Son of God, throw Yourself down from here. For it is written: He shall give His angels charge concerning you, to preserve you, and in their hands, they shall hold you up, lest you strike your foot against a stone. Luke 4:9-11 MEV

Jesus answered him, It is said, You shall not tempt the Lord your God. Luke 4:12 MEV

How Jesus overcame the test – He quoted the Word from Deuteronomy 6:16.

When the devil had ended all the temptations, he departed from Him until another time. Luke 4:13 MEV

This was not the end of all the temptations to sin that the devil would confront Jesus with, but; through this Jesus did overcome all the tests and did not sin, and in due process, showed us how to overcome the devil's temptations, and how to not fall into our enemy's trap of sin.

These three types of temptations are the very same sort of temptations that the devil tempted Eve successfully within the Garden of Eden, as recorded in Genesis 3:1-7, and these same three temptations; each and every one of us will be tempted with as well.

The god of this world has blinded the minds of those who do not believe, lest the light of the glorious gospel of Christ, who is the image of God, should shine on them. II Corinthians 4:4 MEV

Do not love the world or the things in the world. If anyone loves the world, the love of the Father is not in him. For all that is in the world – the lust of the flesh, the lust of the eyes, and the pride of life – is not of the Father, but is of the world. The world and its desires are passing away, but the one who does the will of God lives forever. I John 2:15-17 MEV

Beloved, I implore you as aliens and strangers and exiles [in this world] to abstain from the sensual urges (the evil desires, the passions of the flesh, your lower nature) that wage war against the soul. I Peter 2:11 AMPC

The bad news is we all will be tempted by the god of this world with the things of this world, but; the good news is that the devil doesn't change his tactics, and we can learn from through the study of our Bibles to recognize his tricks and his lies, and thus overcome the same way Jesus did: Take the helmet of salvation and the sword of the Spirit, which is the word of God. Ephesians 6:17 MEV

Be sober and watchful, because your adversary the devil walks around as a roaring lion, seeking whom he may devour. Resist him firmly in the faith, knowing that the same afflictions are experienced by your brotherhood throughout the world. I Peter 5:8-9 MEV

Behold, a very important word of warning here.

Please take special note of this Truth: The deceiver, that is the devil; has had thousands of years to study human behavior, and he knows exactly when and how to come to tempt us. On top of that, the devil knows the Scriptures, and he knows them better that the average Christian does. If you go back to Genesis and carefully read exactly what God said to Adam and Eve in the Garden and then compare what Eve said and what the serpent spoke, you will see that the devil knows what God said, but, he takes the Word and alters it or twists it just enough to render it false and to cast doubt, and doubt is the womb of unbelief. The devil did the very same thing when he was tempting Jesus in the wilderness when he misquoted or attempted to apply portions of the Scripture out of context when tempting Jesus.

We all can expect the devil to use the very same tactics on us, and if we do not know the Scriptures, he could fool you or lead you into fear and doubt; which will ultimately lead to deception and unbelief. The only way not to become a victim of Satan and his deception is to read and study the Word of God every day. It is literally a matter of life and death, and the Word of God is your only offensive weapon.

We shall use this parable to demonstrate how perilous this sort of thing could be.

Let's imagine that you find yourself in a very bad part of town late at night. As you walk along, you are confronted by a gang of armed hoodlums, and it is very apparent that they have every intention to steal your valuables and assault you physically in the worst possible way, and conceivably even kill you. But, you own a 12-gauge shotgun loaded with buckshot at home in your closet. So, you say to the leader of the gang of blood thirsty marauders:

Oh, excuse me Mr. Bad-Actor, I see you have guns and knives, and I too, have a big gun at home in my closet. Now, I must ask you and your associates to stop and wait until I can go home and get my gun and return, and then; we can continue our interaction, okay?

Yeah, right! This is not the real world, is it? If anyone were caught in this life threating situation on the street, there would not be any opportunity to pause the action and retreat to your home or automobile to grab your weapon, and then return to the scene of the crime to engage these attackers. No, if any of us were confronted like this, it would be too late. We would be in very serious distress, perhaps even facing death, depending on the nature of the attack.

This is the same sort of scenario that we all will find ourselves in when we come under an attack from the devil. You can't say: Oh excuse me, Mr. devil; I know you only come to steal, kill, and destroy my family, finances, health and my life. This really isn't fair, and I know I have a Bible somewhere, and I think there could be some Scripture that I can use to resist you with, so; you need to just shut-up now and wait till I can find my Bible and read-up on this, and then you can return and try to steal, kill, and destroy my life.

This surely is not reality, is it? No, simply put; it is too late to fend-off the attacker. The only way to be prepared is to have your weapon with you, which means you must know the Word of God. We cannot fail to communicate this vital fact and not properly amplify this Truth here. Please take heed, if you do not know the Word of God, you will be deceived by the evil one.

So, to review before we continue; after Jesus was Holy Spirit-filled, He was led by the Holy Spirit into the wilderness to deny Himself (die to His flesh-man), and as our example; we too must deny ourselves (die to our flesh-man) in our journey to become just like Jesus and to Imitate Him in every way.

After we chose to deny ourselves (die to our flesh-man) and continue daily to successfully deny our fleshly urges and desires, we advance to the next level of our sanctification and spiritual maturing process by taking up our cross or dying to our soul-man as we follow Jesus. Here, again and always; Jesus is our example in all things.

As Jesus grew in knowledge and wisdom by His study of the Scriptures, Jesus received revelation of who He was and what was His ultimate mission and destiny, which was to die a tortured death on a Roman cross.

Many people believe that to suggest Jesus, the Son of God; had to learn and grow, is blasphemous. Jesus was born of a woman, and Jesus had to develop as a human being just like you and me. In chapter two of Luke's Gospel, we see after Joseph and Mary presenting Jesus to the Lord at the Temple per the Law of Moses and their encounters with Simeon and Anna at the Temple, they took their infant Son and traveled to their home in Galilee, north of Samaria.

When they had performed everything according to the law of the Lord, they returned to Galilee, to their own city of Nazareth. And the Child grew and became strong in spirit, filled with wisdom. And the grace of God was upon Him. Luke 2:39-40 MEV

And then when Jesus was twelve years old, the family came to Jerusalem for the Passover Feast, and to celebrate Jesus' graduation of sorts, because this would have been His Bar mitzvah. (which means Son of the commandments). And it was at this time we see more proof of Jesus' humanity. Our personal belief is that at the Passover Feast was when Jesus received revelation of Himself in the Scriptures, and who He was and what His definitive destiny was coming in His future, and His ministry to the people.

Think about it. Jesus had been studying the Scriptures, and then came to Jerusalem to practice the Scriptures, and to see all the rituals acted out and the Passover Lamb being slain, it is no wonder why He stayed behind to listen, question, and discuss these things with the Rabbis and teachers of the Scriptures. I suspect we might have had a few questions too! Jesus had been there at the Temple for three days when His mom and dad discovered Him. Perhaps these three days that Jesus was "lost" is yet another foreshadowing of Jesus' death and three days in hell. Here was Jesus' response. To His earthly parents:

He said to them, How is it that you searched for Me? Did you not know that I must be about My Father's business? But they did not understand the word which He spoke to them. Luke 2:49-50 MEV

If Jesus was all-knowing, why did He stay behind to listen and ask questions of the teachers in Jerusalem? And if Jesus was all-knowing, why didn't He know His family was upset and searching for Him? Yes, it is obvious that Jesus was a very bright young man, but; He still had to grow-up like every one of us must grow and develop, and Jesus was obedient and submissive to His earthly parents, who didn't know ultimately what was going to happen either.

Then He went down with them and came to Nazareth and was obedient to them. But His mother kept all these words in her heart. And Jesus increased in wisdom and in stature and in favor with God and men. Luke 2:51-52 MEV

Again, if Jesus was all-powerful and all-knowing, how could He increase in wisdom? Stature? Favor? How or why would He need to increase with His Father God and increase in anything with mortal men?

Yes, Jesus was, is, and will always be the Son of God, but; Jesus chose to humble Himself and to strip Himself of all His heavenly stature, power, and privilege to be born of a woman and to walk this earth as the Son of Man and to be tempted in every way, like us. (see Philippians 2:5-11) This is what qualified Him as our Passover Lamb and our Redeemer. Jesus paid the legal ransom required for our sin-debt that we could not pay. Hallelujah! Oh, thank you Jesus.

For even the Son of Man came not to be served, but to serve, and to give His life as a ransom for many. Mark 10:45 MEV

There is one God and one mediator between God and men, the Man Christ Jesus, who gave Himself as a ransom for all. I Timothy 2:5-6a MEV

For you know that you were not redeemed from your vain way of life inherited from your fathers with perishable things, like silver or gold, but with the precious blood of Christ, as of a lamb without blemish and without spot. I Peter 1:18-19 MEV

There are many names and titles for Jesus throughout the Scriptures, (see chapter twenty) but; the one Name that Jesus used over and over when referring to Himself was Son of Man, further emphasizing His humanity.

So, Jesus, the Son of Man; had to go through the process of dying to His soul-man, and He asks and expects this of His disciples too.

We see recorded in the Scriptures, Jesus informing His disciples on more than a dozen different occasions directly and indirectly through parables, how His earthly ministry was going to climax with His death in Jerusalem very soon. But, seemingly, they just didn't get it.

From that time on, Jesus began to show His disciples that He must go to Jerusalem and suffer many things from the elders and chief priests and scribes, and be killed, and be raised on the third day. Matthew 16:21 MEV (Mark 8:31-9:1, Luke 9:22-27)

For He was teaching His disciples, saying, The Son of Man will be delivered into the hands of men, and they will kill Him. After He is killed, He will rise the third day. But they did not understand the teaching and were afraid to ask Him. Mark 9:31-32 MEV (Matthew 17:22-23, Luke 9:43-45)

Taking the twelve, He said, Listen! We are going up to Jerusalem, and everything that is written by the prophets concerning the Son of Man will be accomplished, for He will be handed over to the Gentiles and will be mocked and insulted and spit upon. They will scourge Him and put Him to death, and on the third day He will rise again. They understood none of these things. This saying was hidden from them, and they did not comprehend what was spoken. Luke 18:31-34 MEV (Matthew 20:17-19, Mark 10:32-34)

Jesus answered them, The hour has come for the Son of Man to be glorified. Truly, truly I say to you, unless a grain of wheat falls to the ground and dies, it remains alone. But if it dies, it bears much fruit. He who loves his life will lose it. And he who hates his life in this world will keep it for eternal life. If anyone serves Me, he must follow Me. Where I am, there will

My servant be also. If anyone serves Me, the Father will honor him. John 12:20-26 MEV

Jesus is obviously telling His disciples yet again that He was going to die, and as His servants and followers; He expects the same from them and us.

Now My soul is troubled. What shall I say? Father, save Me from this hour? Instead, for this reason I came to this hour. Father, glorify Your name. John 12:27-28 MEV

We can clearly see Jesus was struggling emotionally with what was rapidly approaching, because it plainly says that His soul is troubled. Jesus knew the horrendous torture, humiliation, and agonizing death on a Roman cross that was his destiny, unless He chose not to endure it.

Finally, we see in those final dark and stressful hours there in the garden of Gethsemane as Jesus is truly dying to His soul-man, and submitting to His Father's will, we have trouble even trying to imagine the incredible struggle Jesus was experiencing in those moments, but; we shall try to go there.

Just think about it, you had been trying to explain to your disciples that you were going to have to be mistreated in the worst possible way and literally die at the hands of the Jews and the Romans, and they,

His disciples; are arguing about their position in the kingdom and who would be the greatest, and who would get the best seat next to your throne.

And you also knew that one of your chosen twelve disciples was going to betray you for a few pieces of silver, and you knew that one of your closest disciples and confidants was going to deny he even knew you multiple times, and all of the remaining ten, except one; would scatter like a bunch of frightened mice.

And you also knew in a few days that you were going to be wrongfully accused of some made-up charges, based on lies, in some bogus court, and then forced to endure multiple illegal "council proceedings" and then to be beaten, slapped, mocked, spit on, and the hair of your head and face to be ripped-out by the handfuls.

Then, you would be forced to go before the Governor of the State and all the people that you had tried to help, with a crown fashioned out of three-inch thorns shoved down your head as those thorns tore through your scalp and ground against your skull. Then the Governor would basically wash his hands of his responsibilities and turn you over to an enraged demonic lynch mob because that was his best move politically.

Then they would judge you and find you "guilty" of some phony crime and sentence you to a slow tortured death on a cross, but; not before they took the time to strip you naked and tie you to a whipping post. Once you were secured there, two men with leather-strapped scourges, tipped with metal and bone fragments, would begin to whip, beat, and tear your back, buttocks, shoulders, and the back of your legs repeatedly until your skin was shredded and ripped-off your body and your flesh looked like mangled meat scraps and your backbone and ribs exposed to view.

Then, they would force you would carry your own cross to the bald hill outside the city called Calvary where soldiers would drive nine-inch iron nails through your wrists and ankles, pinning you to a roughhewn wooden cross, then they would hoist that cross into the air so all could see your final agonizing moments, struggling for life; as you hung from those nails.

As you hang there, you begin to think about how they would watch you, knowing if you didn't die in a few hours another soldier would come and smash your legs breaking your bones so you couldn't push-up anymore to draw air into your lungs, so; your last moments of life would be gasping for air as your heart stops beating because of lack of oxygen, or maybe they would thrust a spear through your side piercing your heart. Either way, it would be the end.

Do you think that you might be stressed-out with all the betrayal, selfish ambition, and lack of faith and courage among your closest friends? If you were facing such torture, knowing you could just walk away; what do you think your stress level would be? I think it is safe to say that without supernatural help, no one could stand-up to that kind of mental trauma. This is where Jesus was in those early morning hours, leading up to His day of passion for you and me. Jesus had to choose. (John 10:14-18, John 12:23-27, John 15:13, Matthew 26:52-54, Romans 5:6-8, Philippians 2:5-11, Hebrews 5:7-9)

Then Jesus came with them to a place called Gethsemane and said to the disciples, Sit here while I go and pray close by. He took with Him Peter and the two sons of Zebedee and began to be sorrowful and troubled. Then He said to them, My soul is very sorrowful, even to death. Wait here, and keep watch with Me. He went a little farther, and falling on His face, He prayed, O My father, if it is possible, let this cup pass from Me, Nevertheless, not as I will, but as You will. Matthew 26:36-39 MEV (see also Mark 14:32-42, Luke 22:39-46)

In doctor Luke's detailed account, the Greek physician (Colossians 4:14); we see that an angel came to give Him strength because of such intense emotional stress and trauma that Jesus was experiencing.

An angel from heaven appeared to Him, strengthening Him. And being in anguish, He prayed more earnestly. And His sweat became like great drops of blood falling down to the ground. Luke 22:43-44 MEV

When is the last time you were under such concentrated mental trauma and emotional anguish and stress that you were literally sweating blood? Jesus endured the ultimate levels of this stress for you and me.

We have had the opportunity to interview Medical professionals and they have explained this condition is called *Hematohidrosis*, and it is caused from extreme physical or emotional stress and severe mental anxiety. Jesus was dying to His soul-man, which again is our mind, will, and emotions. As incredible as this episode was that Jesus chose to endure for all of us, there is yet one more event that Jesus must face. Jesus had one more valley to pass through, the deepest, darkest valley of all, which was truly the ultimate sacrifice for our Lord.

Yes, there is still one more level that Jesus must face. Death of His spirit-man, which is the most grievous of all because it meant separation from the Father, and this drama climaxed there on Golgotha as Jesus hung on the tree, literally becoming a curse for us.

As Jesus hung on the cross, He was accursed of God, and became sin for us, as we see written in the Holy Scriptures: If a man has committed a sin worthy of death and is executed, and you hang him on a tree, then his body must not remain all night on the tree, but you must bury him that day (for he that is hanged is accursed of God) so that your land may not be defiled, which the Lord your God is giving you for an inheritance. Deuteronomy 21:22-23 MEV

Christ has redeemed us from the curse of the law by being made a curse for us – as it is written, Cursed is everyone who hangs on a tree – so that the blessing of Abraham might come on the Gentiles through Jesus Christ, that we might receive the promise of the Spirit through faith. Galatians 3:13-14 MEV

God made Him who knew no sin to be sin for us, that we might become the righteousness of God in Him. II Corinthians 5:21 MEV

Jesus was accursed (doomed to destruction) of God, and for our sake, virtually became sin, so we could be redeemed and reconciled back to good standing with the Father. The penalty for sin is death and by Jesus becoming doomed to destruction as a substitute for our sin, and when Jesus freely yielded His spirit-man unto Father God, Jesus' spirit-man became the substitution for our sin, and Jesus literally went to hell for all mankind's sake.

All of this went on as Jesus hung on that wooden cross. Sin is what separates us from a holy God, and our absolutely perfect and holy heavenly Father cannot even look upon defilement and sin, so; when Jesus became our sin substitute there beaten, bloody, and mangled on the cross; Father God had to look away at that moment and this is when we see Jesus cry out as He hung there suspended between heaven and earth.

Now from the sixth hour until the ninth hour there was darkness over all the land. About the ninth hour Jesus cried out with a loud voice, Eli, Eli, lama sabachthani? Which means, My God, My God, why have You forsaken Me? Matthew 27:45-46 MEV

Throughout the Hebrew Scriptures, we see one of the most used names for God is Elohim, which per Strong's concordance, is used 2,598 times. As an example, every time we see the name God used in Genesis chapter one, it is the Hebrew name Elohim, which is the plural form of EL which is the name God singular. We find it very interesting that the Holy Spirit, who is the Author of the Scriptures, chose to record Jesus' words at this moment in the Hebrew language instead of Greek, and the literal interpretation of Eli is My God singular, not plural. It was at this precise moment when Father God had to turn away from Jesus because Jesus had become the sin of the world. These were Jesus' final words uttered on the cross.

…..It is finished. And He bowed His head and gave up His spirit. John 19:30b MEV

Jesus, the Son of Man; had finished the ultimate act of love, submission, and obedience as He gave up His own spirit-man, and His spirit went to Hades (Greek) or Sheol (Hebrew), which is the place of the dead, for both the righteous (Genesis 37:35, I Samuel 2:6, Psalm 16:10) and wicked (Psalm 31:17, Psalm 73:27).

This place of the dead was where all deceased spirits and souls went (Luke 16:19-31) until Jesus went there and took back the keys to death, hell, and the grave (Revelation 1:18) and He led captivity captive (Ephesians 4:8-10), which is the righteous dead, out of paradise, or Abraham's bosom; and ascended to heaven. Sheol is in the center of the earth and is described as the bottomless pit in Revelation 20:1. The only way it could be "bottomless" is to be in the center of the earth. Jesus prophesied that He would be three days in Sheol or Hades.

For as Jonah was three days and three nights in the belly of the great fish, so will the Son of Man be three days and three nights in the heart of the earth. Matthew 12:40 MEV

Jesus told the repentant thief on the cross (Luke 23:43) that he would be with Him in paradise, and paradise was in Abraham's presence with the other righteous dead in Hades or Sheol, that was separated from the place of torment by a great gulf, (Luke 16:22-26) so no one can pass from one place to the other.

On resurrection morning, Jesus appears to Mary Magdalene to comfort her at the empty tomb in the garden, and He told her: Jesus saith unto her, Mary. She turned herself, and saith unto Him, Rabboni; which is to say Master. Jesus saith unto her, Touch Me not; for I am not yet ascended to My Father: But go to My brethren, and say unto them, I ascend unto My Father, and your Father; and to My God and your God. John 20:16-17 KJV

Here, we can see clearly stated in Jesus' own words that He had not yet ascended to the Father, and it was resurrection morning on the third day. The point of all of this is that Jesus experienced spiritual death and separation from Father God to make it possible for our spirits that are dead to be born-again, and to be alive unto God, through Jesus' sacrifice on the cross, and then Jesus carried our sin and shame to Hades for us. The penalty for sin is death, and someone had to pay the price, so; Jesus went to the place of the dead, so we don't have to.

Jesus paid the ransom price with His own shed blood, and then ascended into the Holy of Holies of the heavenly tabernacle as our great High Priest to apply His own blood to the mercy seat. We suspect that is why Jesus wouldn't allow Mary to touch Him there next to the empty garden tomb because this would have defiled Him as our High Priest before entering the Holy of Holies in heaven.

Jesus had to die spiritually and experience separation from Father God and got to Sheol/Hades which was the place of the dead, (Psalm 49:15, Psalm 86:13, Psalm 89:48) so you and I do not have to. This is called the great exchange: God made Him who knew no sin to be sin for us, that we might become the righteousness of God in Him. II Corinthians 5:21 MEV Wow, now that's some good news right there!

Aren't you thankful today that Jesus finished His mission? Oh, thank you, Lord Jesus.

We will now begin to look at the life and ministry of another Bible character to see if we can detect this very same pattern of denying our flesh-man and dying to our soul-man in the life of another individual that was called and used mightily by the Lord because we too are called to do the same.

This is the Believer's Mandate.

Chapter Thirteen

Follow the pattern

F oundational Truth: We are all called to imitate Jesus in every way.

For I have given you an example, that you should do as I have done to you. Truly, truly, I say to you, a servant is not greater than his master, nor is he who is sent greater than he who sent him. John 13:15-16 MEV

Whoever says he remains in Him ought to walk as He walked. I John 2:6 MEV

As one studies the life of such men like Abraham, Isaac, Jacob, Joseph, Moses, Joshua, David, John the Baptist, Paul and others; you can see this same pattern emerging. To continue our study of this pattern, we shall focus on the life of Saul of Tarsus, and his transformation into the apostle Paul, the bond-servant of Jesus Christ.

When most of us think about the apostle Paul, images of one of his intrepid missions or maybe one of his amazing adventures come to mind, or perhaps one of your favorite epistles or verses that he wrote by inspiration enters your thoughts. But Paul's life certainly did not begin as a disciple, missionary, or New Covenant apostle.

We shall establish first that like many dates of certain historical significant events during the first century, we are not sure of the exact date of such events. As one such example, there is not consensus of the birth year of Jesus, hence there is not agreement on the year of His passion either. Our intent is not to attempt to establish such dates, but to give an approximate time frame, which will serve our purposes within this treatise. In other words, if your study of these events has led you to a different conclusion of the date in question, then we shall respectfully disagree until we can learn the correct date when we all get to our heavenly home. So, if you see a date you disagree with, please don't write me a letter about your research opinions. Now, with that disclaimer of sorts out of the way, we shall begin.

In approximately 5 AD Saul was born a Jew in the city of Tarsus, Cilicia; and was a Roman citizen at birth.

But, apparently in his early years the family relocated to Jerusalem. (Acts 22:3, Acts 22:28, Philippians 3:5-6)

Near 15 AD, Saul was an excellent student and is accepted as a Talmid/disciple of Israel's top Rabbi Gamaliel and was located in Jerusalem. And as was the custom, Saul was dedicated to his studies and to his Rabbi until he too was accepted as Master of the Law in approximately 34 AD, when he is now a Pharisee. Saul was obviously a very zealous man and is actively harassing, molesting, and persecuting men and women of the early Church, acting under the authority of the Great Sanhedrin; and in the name of God.

Saul was present (Acts 7:58) and obviously supportive of the stoning execution of the young preacher of the Gospel named Stephen, (Acts 8:1-3) and continued to violently persecute anyone he could find that was a follower of Jesus. Saul became an authorized agent of the Great Sanhedrin and was given written orders from the high priest to travel to Damascus to search-out these followers of the Way that had fled to that city to escape harassment and possibly death.

It was during this hot pursuit of these disciples of Jesus on the road to Damascus that everything in Saul's world was about to change. (Acts 9:1-19) We all know what happened. Saul had a personal encounter with Jesus Christ, got born-again, was blinded for three days and didn't eat or drink. A devout believer by the name of Ananias was sent by the Lord to Saul to lay hands on Saul for healing and restoration of his sight and for Saul to be filled with the Holy Spirit, the promise of the Father to each one of us.

After a few days, Saul began to preach in the synagogues that Christ is the Son of God. The Jews in Damascus were dumbfounded by Saul at first and didn't know what to do with him, but; after a while they decided the best course of action was to permanently shut him up, so; they plotted to kill him. However, Saul got wind of their evil plans and the disciples there helped Saul escape out of the city by night (Acts 9:23-25), and he returned the one hundred fifty miles back to Jerusalem.

Once Saul returned in Jerusalem, Barnabas tried to help Saul assimilate among the other believers there, but; most were circumspect of him. Saul tried to preach there also and got into a dispute against the Hellenists (Greek cultured religious Jews) and now they too wanted to kill Saul. (Acts 9:26-30) The Church leaders sent Saul back north to Tarsus (four-hundred-mile trek north of Jerusalem) to preserve his life.

With seemingly everyone wanting to kill Saul, he journeyed into (his wilderness season) Arabia and remained there three years. (Galatians 1:10-18) It was during this time that Saul was beginning to be taught by direct revelation the awesome truths we now have recorded in the New Testament epistles. After three years of isolation in Arabia, which was approximately at the end of 37 AD, Saul returns to Jerusalem and he meets with Peter and James for fifteen days, and then he travels back north to Asia Minor for the next ten years of seclusion.

After this decade of years had passed, the Church in Antioch was growing, and the Church in Jerusalem sent Barnabas to Antioch to help and Barnabas traveled to Tarsus to find Saul and to encourage him to come back with him and help preach and teach the growing number of disciples of Christ there also.

Barnabas and Saul remained there in Antioch of Syria for a full year teaching and training disciples. It was at this time that the followers of the Way were first called Christians there in Antioch. (Acts 11:22-26)

A prophet by the name of Agabus prophesied (Acts 11:28) that a great famine was coming upon the entire Roman empire and the Church in Antioch determined to send a relief offering to their brothers in southern Israel, and this financial gift was carried by Barnabas and Saul. After those days, Barnabas and Saul returned to Antioch with a young man by the name of John Mark.

Once Barnabas and Saul returned, the Holy Spirit moved among them and instructed them to be separated and commissioned into a new work. It was then that Barnabas, Saul and John Mark embarked on their first missionary journey throughout Asia Minor in approximately 46-48 AD. (Acts 13:1-3)

There are Bible scholars that will argue these dates and years of the various events, but; we want to simply create a general timeline in your understanding to help us all see that from Saul's famous Damascus road experience until he was called, separated, commissioned, and sent by the Holy Spirit as an apostle/missionary was at least thirteen years. Saul was not called Paul till after this commissioning and activation by the Spirit of the Lord. (Acts 13:9)

The first three years Saul spent in the Arabian wilderness, Saul was dying to his flesh, and the next ten quiet years Saul was dying to his soul. It wasn't till after all this time and many people literally wanting to kill him, was Saul then launched out into the mission field to fulfill his God ordained spiritual destiny and calling.

We all tend to think of Paul as this incredibly bright, talented, and well-educated man that had a great command of the Scriptures that had this awesome encounter with the Lord Jesus on the road to Damascus, and then he was immediately launched out from there into the mission field doing these great exploits for the Lord and in his spare time writing two-thirds of the New Testament, but; that simply was not the situation, and neither will that be the case with anyone else used mightily by the Lord.

Saul was called by the Lord Jesus into the work of the ministry, but; Saul had to die to the lusts of the flesh, and the lusts of the eyes, and the pride of life first in the wilderness of Arabia and Asia Minor before he was ready to be used by the Lord. Saul had to take up his cross and follow Jesus, which meant that had to die to his soul-man with all his plans, thoughts, dreams, and aspirations. After this time of sanctification and consecration unto the Lord, when Saul was dead, then Paul could be a fully committed bond-servant and live to do the works that Jesus Christ had chosen and ordained for him to complete. Even though

Saul was born-again and Spirit-filled, Saul had to choose to submit and deny himself before Jesus Christ could live through Paul.

I have been crucified with Christ. It is no longer I who live, but Christ who lives in me. And the life I now live in the flesh, I live by faith in the Son of God, who loved me and gave Himself for me. Galatians 2:20 MEV

Those that are Christ's have crucified the flesh with its passions and lusts. If we live in the Spirit, let us also walk in the Spirit. Galatians 5:24-25 MEV

Brethren, together follow my example and observe those who live after the pattern we have set for you. Philippians 3:17 AMPC

Follow me as I follow Christ. I Corinthians 11:1 MEV

Saul had to deny his flesh and take up his cross, and then he could be led by the Spirit of God into his true calling, purpose, and destiny. Therefore, just as it was for Paul; so, shall it be for you and me.

This is the Believer's Mandate.

Chapter Fourteen
Authority crisis

Foundational Truth: The world is experiencing an authority crisis because of Bible illiteracy.

What in the world is going on? Has the entire world gone crazy? Does anybody anywhere really know the Truth? Who is in charge of this mess? Do you ever find yourself asking these sorts of questions? So, where do we seek the Truth? Who holds the solutions to our problems?

All the people, families, nations, and kingdoms of the world are in crisis; an authority crisis. All authority is being questioned, challenged, or utterly ignored because people do not know who or what to believe. Nothing seems real anymore and confusion and chaos is the new normal.

Marital authority, Parental authority, Political authority, Governmental authority, Academic authority, and Ecclesiastical or Church authority is all being questioned.

Each of us have experienced this in our lives and can probably site multiple examples of this reality along with the chaos, confusion, anarchy, and unbearable stress that follows all this mass rebellion and self-centered narcissistic behavior. Everyone is doing what seems right to them.

All this dysfunction and lack of recognition of authority leads to a personal identity crisis. Every human on the planet will at some point be confronted with the following questions, and the answers to these questions define our lives and ultimately establish our destinies.

Who am I? Where did I come from? Why am I here? Where am I going? To whom am I accountable? Who or what is my ultimate authority?

The answers to these questions are boiled down and combined to establish our personal identity. Simply stated you must know who you are and whose you are. There is some good news in all of this, and the good news is that in reality there is only one question that must be answered:

Is the Word of God true?

You see, there are only two kingdoms in the world and we all are citizens of one of these two kingdoms: the kingdom of Light and the kingdom of darkness. We must all choose which King and kingdom we shall serve. If you say, "I don't want to choose" then you have in-fact chosen by default, which is darkness.

Okay, we must now return our full attention to the one matter that must be settled: Is the Word of God true? Each one of us as individuals must come to the definitive answer to this question for ourselves. Why? Because everything else in our lives flows from this one decision.

Literally, you are in control of your own eternal and final destination, and your final destiny hangs on this one ultimate decision. The Holy Bible is God's Word and God's will for all mankind forevermore. Do you believe this?

This really is the bottom line, and if you have decided that your answer to the question above is: No, I do not believe that the Holy Bible is God's Word and God's will for me, then we don't have much more to discuss, because we believe the Bible; every single word of it; from Genesis to Revelation.

However, we must conclude that you would not be reading a book about the Scriptures and the Holy Bible if you did not at least have some faith that the Word of God is true.

So, we shall proceed in finding within the Word of God what He has to teach us about this issue of ultimate authority and thus our identity and promises as citizens of His kingdom.

Now, Lord God, You are God, and Your words are true. You have spoken this good message to Your servant. II Samuel 7:28 MEV

It's all about Jesus, our Divine Authority: Savior, Priest, Judge, and King.

I will worship toward Your holy temple and praise Your name for Your loving-kindness and for Your truth and faithfulness; for You have exalted above all else Your name and Your word and You have magnified Your word above all Your name. Psalm 138:2 AMPC

Bless is the man who walks not in the counsel of the ungodly, Nor stands in the path of sinners, Nor sits in the seat of the scoffers; but his delight is in the law of the Lord, and in His law he meditates day and night. He will be like a tree planted by the rivers of water, that brings forth its fruit in its season; its leaf will not wither; And whatever he does will prosper. Psalm 1:1-3 MEV

Your word is true from the beginning, and every one of Your righteous judgements endures forever. Psalm 119:160 MEV

Study this Book of Instruction continually. Meditate on it day and night so you will be sure to obey everything written in it. Only then will you prosper and succeed in all you do. Joshua 1:8 NLT

When people do not accept divine guidance, they run wild. But whoever obeys the law is joyful. Proverbs 29:18 NLT

When the [uncompromisingly] righteous are in authority, the people rejoice; but when the wicked man rules, the people groan and sigh. Proverbs 29:2 AMPC

All has been heard; the end of the matter is: Fear God [revere and worship Him, knowing that He is] and keep His commandments, for this is the whole of man [the full, original purpose of his creation, the object of God's providence, the root of character, the foundation of all happiness, the adjustment to all inharmonious circumstances and conditions under the sun] and the whole [duty] for every man. For God shall bring every work into judgement, with every secret thing, whether it is good or evil. Ecclesiastes 12:13-14 AMPC

But He said, Indeed, blessed are those who hear the word of God and keep it. Luke 11:28 MEV

Understand [this], my beloved brethren. Let every man be quick to hear [a ready listener], slow to speak, slow to take offense and to get angry. For a man's anger does not promote the righteousness God [wishes and requires]. So get rid of all uncleanness and rampant outgrowth of wickedness, and in a humble (gentle, modest) spirit receive and welcome the Word which implanted and rooted [in your hearts] contains the power to save your souls. But be doers of the Word [obey the message], and not merely listeners to it, betraying yourselves [into deception by reasoning contrary to the Truth]. For if anyone only listens to the Word without obeying it and being a doer of it, he is like a man who looks carefully at his [own] natural face in a mirror; For he thoughtfully observes himself, and then goes off and promptly forgets what he was like. But he who looks carefully into the faultless law, the [law] of liberty, and is faithful to it and perseveres in looking into it, being not a heedless listener who forgets but an active doer [who obeys], he shall be blessed in his doing (his life of obedience). James 1:19-25 AMPC

For the Word of God is alive and powerful. It is sharper than the sharpest two-edged sword, cutting between soul and spirit, between joint and marrow. It exposes our innermost thoughts and desires. Nothing in all creation is hidden from God. Everything is naked and exposed before His eyes and He is the one to whom we are accountable. Hebrews 4:12-13 NLT

So Jesus said to those Jews who had believed in Him, If you abide in My word [hold fast to My teaching and live in accordance with them], you are truly My disciples. And you will know the Truth, and the Truth will set you free. John 8:31-32 AMPC

When Jesus had spoken these things, He lifted up His eyes to heaven and said, Father, the hour has come. Glorify and exalt and honor and magnify Your Son, so that Your Son may glorify and extol and honor and magnify You. [Just as] You have granted Him power and authority over all flesh (all humankind), [now glorify Him] so that He may give eternal life to all whom You have given Him. And this is eternal life: [it means] to know (to perceive, recognize, become acquainted with, and understand) You, the only true and real God, and [likewise] to know Him, Jesus [as the] Christ (the Anointed One, the Messiah), Whom You have sent. John 17:1-3 AMPC

Jesus came and told His disciples, I have been given all authority in heaven and on earth. Therefore, go and make disciples of all the nations, baptizing them in the name of the Father and the Son and the Holy

Spirit. Teach these new disciples to obey all the commands I have given you. And be sure of this: I am with you always, even to the end of the age. Matthew 28:18-20 NLT

[Now] He is the exact likeness of the unseen God [the visible representation of the invisible]; He is the Firstborn of all creation. For it was in Him that all things were created, in heaven and on earth, things seen and things unseen, whether thrones, dominions, rulers, or authorities; all things were created and exist through Him [by His service, intervention] and in and for Him. And He Himself existed before all things, and in Him all things consist (cohere, are held together). He also is the Head of [His] body, the church; seeing He is the Beginning, the Firstborn from among the dead, so that He alone in everything and in every respect might occupy the chief place [stand first and be preeminent]. For it has pleased [the Father] that all the divine fullness (the sum total of the divine perfection, powers, and attributes) should dwell in Him permanently. And God purposed that through (by the service, the intervention of) Him [the Son] all things should be completely reconciled back to Himself, whether on earth or in heaven, as through Him, [the Father] made peace by means of the blood of His cross. Colossians 1:15-20 AMPC

We know that a few of these Scripture passages are referenced elsewhere in this book, but; they are so important that they bear repeating because: So then faith comes by hearing, and hearing by the word of God. Romans 10:17 MEV

Jesus has all power, authority, dominion, riches, wisdom, honor, glory, splendor, and blessings forever and ever. Amen. Every believer's mandate in this life is to submit to Jesus, the King of kings and Lord of lords, the ultimate Authority over all things in heaven and earth and beneath the earth.

Here is the bottom line: The world is in an authority crisis because they do not know the Truth, and the Word of God is Truth. We are to first and foremost to believe on Jesus, and then we are to know, believe, obey, and act the Word of God. The Lord God Almighty is the highest, greatest, and ultimate Authority in all things now and forever.

For am I now seeking the approval of men or of God? Or am I trying to please Men? For if I were still trying to please men, I would not be the servant of Christ. Galatians 1:10 MEV

This is the Believer's Mandate.

Chapter Fifteen

Enemies of the cross

Foundational Truth: Today there are many enemies of the cross of Christ within the Church.

Who are the enemies of the cross? And what makes them an enemy? We must discover the answer to these questions to be certain that we do not find ourselves falling into this group of carnal, worldly minded so-called believers in the Church. Yes, in the Church!

I appeal to you, brethren, to be on your guard concerning those who create dissensions and difficulties and cause divisions, in opposition to the doctrine (the teaching) which you have been taught. [I warn you to turn aside from them, to] avoid them. For such persons do not serve our Lord Christ but their own appetites and base desires, and by ingratiating and flattering speech, they beguile the hearts of the unsuspecting and the simpleminded [people]. Romans 16:17-19 AMPC

But even if we or an angel from heaven should preach to you a gospel contrary to and different from that which we preached to you, let him be accursed (anathema, devoted to destruction, doomed to eternal punishment)! As we said before, so I now say again: If anyone is preaching to you a gospel different from or contrary to that which you received [from us], let him be accursed (anathema, devoted to destruction, doomed to eternal punishment)! Galatians 1:8-9 AMPC

But also [in those days] there arose false prophets among the people, just as there will be false teachers among yourselves, who will subtly and stealthily introduce heretical doctrines (destructive heresies), even denying and disowning the Master Who bought them, bringing upon themselves swift destruction. And many will follow their immoral ways and lascivious doings; because of them the true Way will be maligned and defamed. II Peter 2:1-2 AMPC

Beloved, my whole concern was to write to you in regard to our common salvation. [But] I found it necessary and was impelled to write you and urgently appeal to and exhort [you] to contend for the faith which was once for all handed down to the saints [the faith which is that sum of Christian belief which was delivered verbally to the holy people of God]. For certain men have crept in stealthily [gaining entrance secretly by a side door]. Their doom was predicted long ago, ungodly [impious, profane] persons who pervert the grace (spiritual blessing and favor) of our God into lawlessness and wantonness and immorality, and disown and deny our sole Master and Lord, Jesus Christ (the Messiah, the Anointed One). Jude 1:3-4 AMPC

Brethren, together follow my example and observe those who live after the pattern we have set for you. For there are many, of whom I have often told you and now tell you even with tears, who walk (live) as enemies of the cross of Christ (the Anointed One). They are doomed and their fate is eternal misery (perdition); their god is their stomach (their appetites, their sensuality) and they glory in their shame, siding with earthly things and being of their party. Philippians 3:17-19 AMPC

Who are the enemies of the cross? Preachers and teachers that do not preach and teach the whole counsel of God, and they rarely, if ever; confront sin. They are also carnal, worldly minded Christians that claim to be "good church folks" on Sunday, however;

they are living in rebellion and lifestyles full of unrepentant sin and iniquity.

Some of these are Pastors and Elders of churches. Some are deacons, worship ministers, and other lay-leaders within the churches and various denominations and religious groups. Jesus warned us about these false prophets and teachers, and who or what they really serve.

Remember false prophets and teachers are real prophets and real teachers that preach and teach falsehoods, and do not teach the people the unadulterated Truth.

Sanctify them by Your truth. Your word is truth. John 17:17 MEV

Now the serpent was more subtle and crafty than any living creature of the field which the Lord God had made. And he [satan] said to the woman, Can it really be that God has said, You shall not eat from every tree of the garden? Genesis 3:1 AMPC

Your prophets have predicted for you falsehood and delusion and foolish things; and they have not exposed your iniquity and guilt to avert your captivity [by causing you to repent]. But they have divined and declared to you false and deceptive prophecies, worthless and misleading. Lamentations 2:14 AMPC

There is a conspiracy of [Israel's false] prophets in the midst of her, like a roaring lion tearing the prey; they have devoured human lives; they have taken [in their greed] treasure and precious things; they have made widows in the midst of her. Her priests have done violence to My law and have profaned holy things. They have made no distinction between the sacred and the secular, neither have they taught people the difference between the unclean and the clean and have hid their eyes from My Sabbaths, and I am profaned among them. Her princes in the midst of her are like wolves rending and devouring the prey, shedding blood and destroying lives to get dishonest gain. And her prophets have daubed them over with whitewash, seeing false visions and divining lies to them, saying, Thus says the Lord God – when the Lord has not spoken. Ezekiel 22:25-28 AMPC

Beware of false prophets, who come to you dressed as sheep, but inside they are devouring wolves. Matthew 7:15 AMPC

Jesus answered them, Be careful that no one misleads you [deceiving you and leading you into error]. For many will come in (on the strength of) My name [appropriating the name which belongs to Me], saying, I am the Christ (the Messiah), and they will lead many astray. And many false prophets will rise up and deceive and lead many into error. And the love of the great body of people will grow cold because of the multiplied lawlessness and iniquity, But he who endures to the end will be saved. Matthew 24:4-5, 11-13 AMPC

These people are deceived. They call themselves Christians and claim to follow the Lord Jesus, however; they are living for themselves and their desires because their love for the Lord and His Church has grown cold. What's worse is that they are leading others into deception in the process.

These people believe in the concept of Jesus, but; they don't believe Jesus and obey His Word. We are called to live totally surrendered, submitted lives as bond-servants to our Master. Jesus teaches that we must lay down our plans, wants, wills, and desires and follow Him. Jesus must be first in all things.

If anyone comes to Me and does not hate his [own] father and mother [in the sense of indifference to or relative disregard for them in comparison with his attitude toward God] and [likewise] his wife and children and brothers and sisters – [yes] and even his own life also- he cannot be My disciple. Whoever does not persevere and carry his own cross and come after (follow) Me cannot be My disciple. Luke 14:26-27 AMPC

And Jesus called [to Him] the throng with His disciples and said to them, If anyone intends to come after Me, let him deny himself [forget, ignore, disown, and lose sight of himself and his own interests] take up his cross, and [joining Me as a disciple and siding with My party] follow with Me [continually, cleaving steadfastly to Me]. For whoever wants to save his [higher, spiritual, eternal] life, will lose it [the lower, natural, temporal life which is lived only on earth]; and whoever gives up his life [which is lived only on earth] for My sake and the Gospel's will save it [his higher, spiritual life in the eternal kingdom of God]. Mark 8:34-35 AMPC

Someone said to Him, Listen! Your mother and Your brothers are standing outside, seeking to speak to You. But He replied to the man who told Him, Who is My mother, and who are My brothers? And stretching out His hand toward [not only the twelve disciples but all] His adherents, He said, Here are My mother and My brothers. For whoever does the will of My Father in heaven is My brother and sister and mother! Matthew 12:47-50 AMPC

Therefore, everyone who acknowledges Me before men and confesses Me [out of a state of oneness with Me], I will also acknowledge him before My Father Who is in heaven and confess [that I am abiding in] him. But whoever denies and disowns Me before men, I also will deny and disown him before My Father Who is in heaven. Do not think that I have come to bring peace upon the earth; I have not come to bring peace, but a sword. For I have come to part asunder a man from his father, and a daughter from her mother, and a newly married wife from her mother-in-law. And a man's foes will be they of his own household. He who loves [and takes more pleasure in] father or mother more than [in] Me is not worthy of Me; and he who loves [and takes more pleasure in] son or daughter more than [in] Me is not worthy of Me; And he who does not take up his cross and follow Me [cleaving steadfastly to Me, conforming wholly to My example in living and, if need be, in dying also] is not worthy of Me. Matthew 10:32-38 AMPC

Anyone who loves his life loses it, but anyone who hates his life in this world will keep it to life eternal. [Whoever has on love for, no concern for, no regard for his life here on earth, but despises it, preserves his life forever and ever.] If anyone serves Me, he must continue to follow Me [to cleave steadfastly to Me, conform wholly to My example in living and, if need be, in dying] and wherever I am, there will My servant be also. If anyone serves Me, the Father will honor him. John 12:25-26 AMPC

Therefore Jesus also suffered and died outside the [city's] gate in order that He might purify and consecrate the people through [the shedding of] His own blood and set them apart as holy [for God]. Let us then go forth [from all that would prevent us] to Him outside the camp [at Calvary], bearing the contempt and abuse and shame with Him. Hebrews 13:12-13 AMPC

And they have overcome (conquered) him by the means of the blood of the Lamb and the utterance of their testimony, for they did not love and cling to life even when faced with death [holding their lives cheap till they had to die for their witnessing]. Revelation 12:11 AMPC

Why are these people enemies of the cross? Because they do not want to surrender their will and their desires to the Lordship of Jesus. They will not deny themselves and take up their cross and follow Jesus!

These individuals want to make their own plans and then ask the Lord to bless their plan. They think they are very spiritual because they attend church services and claim to believe in Jesus and are busy doing good things. They have been falsely led to believe that this is what it means to be a real disciple of Christ, or a Christian. These people know about Jesus, but; they don't know Him intimately or His Word assuredly, and both are required to have abiding faith in Him and His Word.

Jesus was speaking specifically of these misguided and deceived people when He said:

Why do you call Me, Lord, Lord, and do not [practice] what I tell you? Luke 6:46 AMPC

Not everyone who says to Me, Lord, Lord, will enter the kingdom of heaven, but he who does the will of My Father Who is in heaven. Many will say to Me on that day, Lord, Lord, have we not prophesied in Your name and driven out demons in Your name and done many mighty works in Your name? And then I will say to them openly (publicly), I never knew you; depart from Me, you who act wickedly [disregarding My commands]. Matthew 7:21-23 AMPC

Jesus makes this very clear and simple for us. This is not complicated (the world makes it complex) and Jesus taught us to follow His example of living and walking in love, and He made certain His will for us was written down so we can study anytime we desire to hear from Him.

Hear, O Israel: the Lord our God is one Lord [the only Lord]. And you shall love the Lord your God with all your [mind and] heart and with your entire being and with all your might. Deuteronomy 6:4-5 AMPC

You shall not take revenge or bear any grudge against the sons of your people, but you shall love your neighbor as yourself. I am the Lord. Leviticus 19:18 AMPC

Teacher, which kind of commandment is great and important (the principal kind) in the Law? [Some commandments are light- which are heavy?] And He replied to him, You shall love the Lord your God with all your heart and with all your soul and with all your mind (intellect). This is the great (most important, principal) and first commandment. And a second is like it: You shall love your neighbor as [you do] yourself. These two commandments sum up and upon them depend all the Law and the Prophets. Matthew 22:37-40 AMPC

We have heard some deceived and misguided teachers of the Word of God that think they are spiritually mature say that this is "Old Testament Law and those Scriptures are not for us New Covenant believers today". Well, here is the Truth: The Holy Spirit inspired apostle Paul to bear witness to these words of Jesus when writing the New Testament epistle of instruction to the church in Rome:

Keep out of debt and owe no man anything, except to love one another; for he who loves his neighbor [who practices loving others] has fulfilled the Law [relating to one's fellowmen, meeting all its requirements]. Romans 13:8 AMPC

Love does no wrong to one's neighbor [it never hurts anybody]. Therefore love meets all the requirements and is the fulfilling of the Law. Romans 13:10 AMPC

And the Holy Spirit moved James, the half-brother of Jesus; to write in his New Testament epistle:

If indeed you [really] fulfill the royal Law in accordance with the Scripture, You shall love your neighbor as [you love] yourself, you do well. James 2:8 AMPC

You believe that there is one God; you do well. The demons also believe and tremble. James 2:19 MEV

Jesus said that all His teaching, instructions, and all His Word is summed-up in the great commandment: The Law of Love which is to love God and love others, which begs the next question; how then do we truly love Him?

If you [really] love Me, you will keep (obey) My commands. John 14:15 AMPC

Jesus answered, If a person [really] loves Me, he will keep My word [obey My teaching]; and My Father will love him, and We will come to him and make Our home (abode, special dwelling place) with him. Anyone who does not [really] love Me does not observe and obey My teaching. And the teaching which you hear and heed is not Mine, but [comes] from the Father Who sent Me. John 14:23-24 AMPC

I have loved you, [just] as the Father has loved Me; abide in My love [continue in His love with Me]. If you keep My commandments [if you continue to obey My instructions], you will abide in My love and live on in it, just as I have obeyed My Father's commandments and live on in His love. John 15:9-10 AMPC

Whoever says, I know Him [I perceive, recognize, understand, and become better acquainted with Him] but fails to keep and obey His commandments (teachings) is a liar, and the Truth [of the Gospel] is not in him. But he who keeps (treasures) His Word [who bears in mind His precepts, who observes His message in its entirety], truly in him has the love of and for God been perfected (completed, reached maturity). By this we may perceive (know, recognize, and be sure) that we are in Him: Whoever says he abides in Him ought [as a personal debt] to walk and conduct himself in the same way in which He walked and conducted Himself. I John 2:4-6 AMPC

By this we come to know (recognize and understand) that we love the children of God: when we love God and obey His commands (orders, charges) - [when we keep His ordinances and are mindful of His precepts and His teaching]. For the [true] love of God is this: that we do His commands [keep His ordinances and are mindful of His precepts and teaching]. And these orders of His are not irksome (burdensome, oppressive, or grievous). I John 5:2-3 AMPC

And what this love consists in is this: that we live and walk in accordance with and guided by His commandments (His orders, ordinances, precepts, teaching). This is the commandment, as you have heard from the beginning, that you continue to walk in love [guided by it and following it]. II John 1:6 AMPC

Hasn't Jesus detailed our responsibility in our relationship with Him in very clear terms? We love Jesus by and through obedience to all His Word. If anyone says that they love the Lord, however; they are not obeying all His Word, then God says that individual is a liar and the Truth is not in that person.

Is this learning to love easy? Yes, we just walk in the Light that we have and as we receive more Light, we walk in that. So, we shall always be growing and applying more Truth and Light to our life because Jesus is Light (John 8:12), and we are called to be Light. (I Thessalonians 5:5)

[So] if we say we are partakers together and enjoy fellowship with Him when we live and move and are walking about in darkness, we are [both] speaking falsely and do not live and practice the Truth [which the Gospel presents]. But if we [really] are living and walking in the Light, as He [Himself] is in the Light, we have [true, unbroken] fellowship with one another, and the blood of Jesus Christ His Son cleanses (removes) us from all sin and guilt [keeps us cleansed from sin in all its forms and manifestations]. I John 1:6-7 AMPC

As we follow Jesus and become increasingly more and more like Him, we must not be shocked when we receive the same sort of response from the world, of which we are foreigners; that Jesus received.

If the world hates you, know that it hated Me before it hated you. If you belonged to the world, the world would treat you with affection and would love you as its own. But because you are not of the world [no longer one with it], but I have chosen (selected) you out of the world, the world hates (detests) you. Remember that I told you, a servant is not greater than his master [is not superior to him]. If they persecuted Me, they will also persecute you; if they kept My word and obeyed My teachings, they will also keep and obey yours. John 15:18-20 AMPC

Indeed all who delight in piety and are determined to live a devoted and godly life in Christ Jesus will meet with persecution [will be made to suffer because of their religious stand]. II Timothy 3:12 AMPC

When they had preached the good news (Gospel) to that town and made disciples of many of the people, they went back to Lystra and Iconium and Antioch, Establishing and strengthening the souls and hearts of the disciples, urging and warning them to stand firm in the faith, and [telling them] that it is through many hardships and tribulations we must enter the kingdom of God. Acts 14:21-22 AMPC

[After all] what kind of glory [is there in it] if, when you do wrong and are punished for it, you take it patiently? But if you bear patiently with suffering [which results] when you do right and that is undeserved, it is acceptable and pleasing to God. For even to this were you called [it is inseparable from your vocation]. For Christ also suffered for you, leaving you [His personal] example, so that you should follow His footsteps. I Peter 2:20-21 AMPC

Take [with me] your share of the hardships and suffering [which you are called to endure] as a good (first class) soldier of Christ Jesus. II Timothy 2:3 AMPC

For that (Gospel) I am suffering affliction and even wearing chains like a criminal. But the Word of God is not chained or imprisoned! Therefore I [am ready to] persevere and stand my ground with patience and endure everything for the sake of the elect [God's chosen], so that they too may obtain [the] salvation which is in Christ Jesus, with [the reward of] eternal glory. The saying is sure and worthy of confidence: If we have died with Him, we shall also live with Him. If we endure, we shall also reign with Him. If we deny and disown and reject Him, He will also deny and disown and reject us. II Timothy 2:9-12 AMPC

For whoever is ashamed [here and now] of Me and My words in this adulterous (unfaithful) and [preeminently] sinful generation, of him will the Son of Man also be ashamed when He comes in the glory (splendor and majesty) of His Father with the holy angels. Mark 8:38 AMPC

I, John, your brother and companion (sharer and participator) with you in the tribulation and kingdom and patient endurance [which are] in Jesus Christ, was on the isle called Patmos, [banished] on account

The Believer's Mandate

of [my witnessing to] the Word of God and the testimony (the proof, the evidence) for Jesus Christ. Revelation 1:9 AMPC

And someone asked Him, will only a few be saved (rescued, delivered from the penalties of the last judgment, and made partakers of the salvation by Christ)? And He said to them, Strive to enter by the narrow door [force yourselves through it], for many, I tell you, will try to enter and will not be able. Luke 13:23-24 AMPC

Enter through the narrow gate; for wide is the gate and spacious and broad is the way that leads away to destruction, and many are those who are entering through it. But the gate is narrow (contracted by pressure) and the way is straightened and compressed that leads away to life, and few are those who find it. Matthew 7:13-14 AMPC

As you can see in the Scriptures, we are all commanded to live unselfish, surrendered lives as we love our Lord Jesus by living in total submission and obedience to His Word, His will, and His ways.

This is the narrow gate Jesus spoke of that few find. Do you believe the Word of God is Truth?

Now we know and believe that the narrow gate is living a Jesus loving, self-sacrificing life, totally yielded to the Word of God. So, what would the wide gate look

Enemies Of The Cross

like? We know because we have apostle Paul's prophecies recorded in his letters to Timothy, forecasting the last days before the return of Jesus. We are now living those days the Holy Spirit told us were coming:

But the [Holy] Spirit distinctly and expressly declares that in latter times some will turn away from the faith, giving attention to deluding and seducing spirits and doctrines that demons teach, through the hypocrisy and pretensions of liars whose consciences are seared (cauterized), who forbid people to marry and [teach them] to abstain from [certain kinds of] foods which God created to be received with thanksgiving by those who believe and have [an increasingly clear] knowledge of the truth. I Timothy 4:1-3 AMPC

This warning in the Word is about the various religious denominations, sects, and cults that have divided and deceived the generations and the body of Christ through the centuries of years and continue to create division and strife within the Church even now. (There are roughly thirty thousand different religious organizations just in the USA alone.)

So for the sake of your tradition (the rules handed down by your forefathers), you have set aside the Word of God [depriving it of force and authority and making it of no effect]. Matthew 15:6 AMPC (see also Mark 7:1-23)

Simply stated, you will not find Adventists, Anglicans, Assemblies of God, Baptists, Catholics, Church of Christ, Dutch Reformed, Eastern Orthodox, Episcopalians, Foursquare, Lutherans, Methodists, Mormons, Oneness, Oriental Orthodox, Pentecostals, Presbyterians, Quakers, Unitarians, etc., or any other such thing in the Word of God.

These are all man-made tradition. Obviously, this list of denominations and religious groups is not exhaustive but intended to simply stress the point that all denominations are man-made and not ordained by God within the Scriptures. If we didn't include your preferred religious tradition in this concise list, we sincerely apologize and will say that your tradition is just as man-made as the rest of the ones listed.

No person will be saved by their good works and deeds or by their membership, participation, or contributions to any social do-gooder's club, denomination, ministry group, or organization. (Isaiah 64:6, Galatians 2:16, Ephesians 2:8-9, II Timothy 1:8-10, Titus 3:4-7) We will be saved by and through our faith in Jesus Christ and His finished work on the cross, and his resurrection from the grave.

But understand this, that in the last days will come (set in) perilous times of great stress and trouble [hard to deal with and hard to bear]. For people will be lovers of self and [utterly] self-centered, lovers of money and aroused by an inordinate [greedy] desire for wealth, proud and arrogant and contemptuous boasters. They will be abusive (blasphemous, scoffing), disobedient to parents, ungrateful, unholy and profane. [They will be] without natural [human] affection (callous and inhuman), relentless (admitting of no truce or appeasement); [they will be] slanderers (false accusers, troublemakers), intemperate and loose in morals and conduct, uncontrolled and fierce, haters of good. [They will be] treacherous [betrayers], rash, [and] inflated with self-conceit. [They will be] lovers of sensual pleasures and vain amusements more than and rather than lovers of God. For [although] they hold a form of piety (true religion), they deny and reject and are strangers to the power of it [their conduct belies the genuineness of their profession]. Avoid [all] such people [turn away from them]. II Timothy 3:1-5 AMPC

(A comprehensive word study on this passage of Scripture follows in chapter sixteen)

Who are the many going through the wide gate that leads away to destruction? They are the enemies of the cross. They are lovers of self and lovers of money. Haters of good. They love their carnal pleasures and worthless entertainments rather than love God. These selfish people despise self-denial. These folks are in the Church, but; they look and act just like the rest of the egocentric world, and many pastors and preachers have gotten so backslidden themselves that they are letting more and more of the world creep into the Church. Of course, this is leading to the great apostasy or the great falling away (II Thessalonians 2:1-3) prophesied to occur just before the antichrist steps upon the world stage of geopolitics. A short definition of apostasy is rebellion or can be simply defined as the abandonment of the Truth.

These individuals claim to love the Lord, but; they have not submitted to the authority of the Word of God. They walk and live by their own plans and pursuits. In summary: Enemies of the cross are the lord of their life.

Jesus has clearly commanded us all to put Him and His agenda first and foremost in our lives, and when we do this; He is faithful to take care of all our needs. Thus, we are never to worry or fret about our future.

But seek (aim at and strive after) first of all His kingdom and His righteousness (His way of doing and being right), and then all these things taken together will be given you besides. So do not worry or be anxious about tomorrow, for tomorrow will have worries and anxieties of its own. Sufficient for each day is its own trouble. Matthew 6:33-34 AMPC

One final question to ask ourselves: How could anyone possibly hope to obey God's will and His way of doing things, if they don't know what His will is?

Well, simply stated, you can't. It is our responsibility to read and meditate on the Word of God day and night in the reverential fear of the Lord, and as we do this consistently; we shall renew our minds and will then see and know the will of God for our lives.

This is the Believer's Mandate.

Chapter Sixteen

Perilous times are here

Foundational Truth: We are in the last days because perilous times and perilous men and women are here now.

This is a continuance of a portion of the previous chapter exposing the enemies of the cross, and this passage of prophetic Scripture gives us more than twenty of the attitudes, behaviors, and characteristics of many people in our society in the last days leading up to the end of the age and the return of Jesus Christ.

Therefore, to gain greater clarity of these individual characteristics and behaviors that we are instructed to be looking for and commanded to turn away from, we shall attempt to gain understanding from conducting a deeper and more comprehensive study of these Holy

Spirit inspired words from the Greek language of the original transcripts as first written.

II Timothy 3:1-5 KJV This know also, that in the last days perilous times shall come. For men shall be lovers of their own selves, covetous, boasters, proud, blasphemers, disobedient to parents, unthankful, unholy, without natural affection, trucebreakers, false accusers, incontinent, fierce, despisers of those that are good, traitors, heady, highminded, lovers of pleasures more than lovers of God; having a form of godliness, but denying the power thereof: from such turn away.

Last (53x Greek) *Eschatos:* end, last, extreme, final, uttermost. This Greek word is the root word of *Eschatology* which is the study of last things, and more specifically; the study of Bible prophecy relating to end-times and/or the end of the age. (John 6:39, 40, 44)

Perilous (2x Greek) *Chalepos:* hard to bear, violent, troublesome, harsh, fierce, dangerous, savage; fiercely difficult to cope with because so harsh, even injurious. (Matthew 8:28)

Lovers of self (1x Greek) *Philautos:* selfish, self-loving; describing someone preoccupied with their own selfish desires and self-interests. Vain and narcissistic (used only here)

Covetous (2x Greek) *Philarguros:* loving money, avaricious; someone literally in love with personal gain and having money or the things money can provide. (Luke 16:14)

Boasters (2x Greek) *Alazon:* vagabond, imposter, braggart; person claims many things he can't do, so he must always keep moving on to new, naïve listeners. (Romans 1:30)

Proud (5x Greek) *Huperephanos:* arrogant, disdainful, haughty; showing oneself above others, despising others or even treating them with contempt, trying to be more than what God directs, going beyond the faith He imparts. (Luke 1:51, Romans 1:30, James 4:6, I Peter 5:5)

Blasphemers (4x Greek) *Blasphemos:* slanderous, evil-speaking, revilers, reproachful, railing, abusive; one who reverses spiritual and moral realities. (Acts 6:11, I Timothy 1:13, II Peter 2:11)

Disobedient (6x Greek) *Apeithes:* Unbelieving, unpersuadable, uncompliant; literally unwilling to be persuaded by God, outward spiritual rebellion, willful unbelief. (Luke 1:17, Acts 26:19, Romans 1:30, Titus 1:16, Titus 3:3)

Unthankful (2x Greek) *Acharistos:* ungracious, ungrateful, unpleasing, thankless. (Luke 6:36)

Unholy (2x Greek) *Anosios:* profane, impious, wicked; without reverence for what should be hallowed, utter disrespect of the things of God. (I Timothy 1:9)

Unloving (2x Greek) *Astorgos:* lacking natural affection; hard-hearted and cold towards kindred. (Romans 1:31)

Trucebreakers (1x Greek) *Aspondos:* unforgiving, unable to please, irreconcilable; not to be bound by treaty or truce. (used only here)

False accusers (38x Greek) *Diabolos:* the devil, slanderous, defamatory, accusing falsely, backbiter, malicious gossips; unjustly criticizing to hurt and malign others, and/or condemns to sever relationships. (John 8:44, Acts 13:10, Ephesians 4:27, Ephesians 6:11, I Timothy 3:6-7, I Timothy 3:11, II Timothy 2:26, Titus 2:3, Hebrews 2:14, James 4:7, I Peter 5:8, I John 3:8-10, Jude 1:9, Revelation 2:10, Revelation 12:9, Revelation 12:12, Revelation 20:2,10)

Incontinent (1x Greek) *Akrates:* lacks self-control, powerless, inclined to excessiveness, no self-restraint. (used only here)

Fierce (1x Greek) *Anemerous:* not tame, savage, brutal, violent. (used only here)

Despisers of good (1x Greek) *Aphilagathos:* without love of good, hater of good; hostile to the things of God, opposed to goodness and those that are good. (used only here)

Traitors (3x Greek) *Prodotes:* betrayer, treacherous. (Luke 6:16, Acts 7:52)

Heady (2x Greek) *Propetes*: impulsive, rash, reckless, thoughtless, wild, unbridled passion. (Acts 19:36)

Highminded (3x Greek) *Tuphoo:* inflated with self-conceit, foolish, vanity, puffed-up; having a muddled mind-set, moral blindness resulting from poor judgement which brings further loss of spiritual perception. (I Timothy 3:6, I Timothy 6:4)

Lovers of pleasure (1x Greek) *Philedonos:* sensuous pleasure-lover, voluptuous; the satisfaction of bodily desires, lusts, and physical appetites at the expense of other things. (used only here)

Perilous Times Are Here

II Timothy 3:5 KJV Having a form of godliness, but denying the power thereof: from such turn away.

Form (2x Greek) *Morphosis:* outline, semblance, appearance, embodiment. (Romans 2:20)

Godliness (15x Greek) *Eusebeia:* piety, radical devotion, reverence, holiness; someone's inner heart response to the things of God which displays itself in and by honor and reverence for God and everything He calls sacred and worthy of veneration. Christ-likeness. (Acts 3:12, I Timothy 2:2, 3:16, 4:7, 4:8, 6:3, 6:5, 6:6, 6:11, Titus 1:1, II Peter 1:3, 1:6, 1:7, 1:11)

Denying (33x Greek) *Arneomai:* not to accept, repudiate, contradict, disown; to reject and refuse to affirm or to confess. (Matthew 10:33, Acts 3:14, Acts 7:35, Titus 2:12, Revelation 2:13)

Power (120x Greek) *Dunamis:* miraculous power, force, might, ability, strength; power through God's ability, power to achieve by applying the Lord's inherent abilities. (Matthew 6:13, Luke 9:1, Acts 1:8, Acts 10:38, Romans 1:4, 1:16, 1:20, 15:19, I Corinthians 1:18, 1:24, 2:4, 2:5, 4:19, 4:20)

Turn away (1x Greek) *Apotrepo:* to avoid, turn away from, shun, deflect. (used only here)

[Word study tools and reference resource library: Strong's Exhaustive Concordance, HELPS Word-studies, NAS Exhaustive Concordance, and Thayer's Greek Lexicon.]

With this prophetic passage the Holy Spirit is very specifically preparing us all for the behavior and heart condition of many in the last days. We believe as each of us consider these various characteristics, no doubt individuals, circumstances, or perhaps news headlines will come to your mind.

Can there be any doubt that we are seeing the fulfillment of Bible prophecy right before our eyes, and we are to be actively watching and praying for the soon return of our Lord and King.

This is the Believer's Mandate.

Chapter Seventeen

Sin in the camp!

Foundational Truth: The Word of God has instructions on how to deal with sin issues within the body of Christ.

However, brothers and sisters; there is sin in the camp!

The previous three chapters we have discussed the lack of respect for authority and the rampant iniquity and sin not just in society but also within the Church. We desperately need instruction on Church discipline and correction in accordance with the Word of God.

Our world is a chaotic place and sometimes it looks and feels like darkness is winning, however; we as children of God can gather together and recharge our batteries, so-to-speak, through the encouraging words and loving fellowship within our own company of brothers and sisters in Christ. This is, of course; is one of the primary reasons we are to gather together often and on a consistent basis.

We must all remind ourselves that the people of the world are ignorant of the things of God and that "sinners sin" and we should never be amazed or discouraged by that fact, nevertheless; we also should be able to reasonably suppose and presume that a gathering of God's people in the name of our Lord Jesus to be comparatively "sin free zones" where we can and should reasonably expect folks not to be living and participating in blatant and unrepentant sinful behavior and lifestyles.

Do not be deceived: "Bad company corrupts good morals." Awake to righteousness and do not sin, for some do not have the knowledge of God. I say this to your shame. I Corinthians 15:33-34 MEV

It is with a heavy heart that we write these words, but; the fact is that many of the Christian congregations and assemblies today look and act just like the carnal world. Children of God, this should not be so because we are the *Ekklesia:* the called-out ones; the Church, the body of Jesus Christ in the earth.

There isn't any doubt that there is a vast array of detailed causes for this lack of holiness in the body of

Sin In The Camp!

Christ today, and much could be said about that subject matter, however; we shall endeavor our focus on searching the Scriptures for God's will on this issue of sinful behavior in the midst of the camp among His called-out people.

We also must carefully study His instructions on how we are commanded to bring correction to those individuals that are involved in ungodly behavior and sinful lifestyles, yet they profess to be true Christians. This is an abomination to Jesus and a reproach to His Church.

We shall begin with the instructions Father God gave to Moses and Joshua, and then follow with the New Testament Scriptures that bear witness to these Truths.

We are the called-out ones! What are we called out of? The world and the sin thereof.

And the Lord spoke to Moses, saying: Speak to all the congregation of the children of Israel, and say to them: You shall be holy, for I the Lord your God am holy. Leviticus 19:1-2 MEV

You shall be holy unto Me; for I the Lord am holy and have separated you from other peoples, that you should be Mine. Leviticus 20:26 MEV

Therefore be perfect, even as your Father who in heaven is perfect. Matthew 5:48 MEV just as He chose us in Him before the foundation of the world, to be holy and blameless before Him in love; Therefore be imitators of God as dear children. Ephesians 1:4, 5:1 MEV

You adulterers and adulteresses, do you not know that friendship with the world is enmity with God? Whoever therefore will be a friend of the world is the enemy of God. James 4:4 MEV

As obedient children do not conduct yourselves according to the former lusts in your ignorance. But as He who has called you is holy, so be holy in all your conduct, because it is written, "Be holy, for I am holy." I Peter 1:14-16 MEV

Do not love the world or the things in the world. If anyone loves the world, the love of the Father is not in him. I John 2:15 MEV

How did Father God instruct His people to deal with false prophets, apostates, and the transgressors of His covenant that was in the midst of the camp?

God's people were commanded to purge evil from the congregation and remove those committing sin or enticing others to sin from among them, after they had investigated to make certain these accusations were true and confirmed by two or more eye witnesses to the transgression. Read: Deuteronomy 13:1-18, Deuteronomy 17:1-7, and Joshua 7:1-26

The hands of the witnesses shall be first against him to put him to death, and afterward the hands of all the people. So you shall purge the evil from among you. Deuteronomy 17:7 MEV

To summarize these three passages of Scripture, Father God clearly expects His covenant people to remain separated from the corrupt world system, and He required that the individuals responsible for the ungodly behavior to be removed from the assembly of His people. Our Omnipotent (Almighty) Omnipresent (Ever-present) and Omniscient (All-knowing) Creator knows that if sin is left alone and not dealt with expeditiously, it shall only grow worse, creating confusion, and ultimately spreading to others.

Jesus Christ has given His Church very clear step-by-step instructions on how we must deal with the offending and/or sinning sister or brother within the local church.

Step #1 - If your brother wrongs you, go and show him his fault, between you and him privately. If he listens to you, you have won back your brother.

Step #2 - But if he does not listen, take along with you one or two others, so that every word may be confirmed and upheld by the testimony of two or three witnesses.

Step #3 - If he pays no attention to them [refusing to listen and obey], tell it to the church;

Step #4 - and if he refuses to listen even to the church, let him be to you as a pagan and a tax collector. Matthew 18:15-17 AMPC

This is such an incredibly important topic that sadly most local churches do not practice consistently, or some choose to ignore this command of Jesus completely. Is it any wonder why there is so much sin, iniquity, and discord in and among the Church today?

I wrote to you in my letter not to keep company with sexually immoral people. Yet I did not mean the sexually immoral people of this world, or the covetous, or extortioners, or the idolaters, since you would then need to go out of the world. But I have written to you not to keep company with any man who is called a brother, who is sexually immoral, or covetous, or an idolater, or a reviler, or a drunkard, or an extortioner. Do not even eat with such a person. For what have I to do with judging those also who are outside? Do you not judge those who are inside? But God judges those that are outside. Therefore "put away from among yourselves that wicked person." I Corinthians 5:9-13 MEV

Do you not know that the unrighteous will not inherit the kingdom of God? Do not be deceived. Neither the sexually immoral, nor idolaters, nor adulterers, nor male prostitutes, nor homosexuals, nor thieves, nor covetous, nor drunkards, nor revilers, nor extortioners will inherit the kingdom of God. Such were some of you. But you were washed, but you were sanctified, and you were justified in the name of the Lord Jesus by the Spirit of our God. I Corinthians 6:9-11 MEV

Brothers and sisters, do not be deceived. The unrighteous will not inherit the kingdom of God:

Sexually immoral (10x Greek) *Pornos:* a fornicator, whoremonger, an individual who prostitutes themselves.

Covetous (4x Greek) *Pleonektes:* a covetous or avaricious person. One desirous of having more. A greedy rapacious person wanting what belongs to others.

Idolater (7x Greek) *Eidololatres:* an image worshiper. Participant in any way in the heathen worship of false gods. Mammon worshipper.

Revilers (2x Greek) *Loidoros:* a railer, abuser. Reproach; used of injuring another's reputation by denigrating, abusive insults. Slanderers.

Drunkards (2x Greek) *Methusos:* drunken, intoxicated.

Extortioners (5x Greek) *Harpax:* rapacious, ravenous, a swindler. Seizing; a sudden snatching.

Adulterers (3x Greek) *Moichos:* an adulterer, apostate. Faithless towards God, ungodly.

Male Prostitutes (4x Greek) *Malakos:* soft, delicate, effeminate. A male who submits his body to unnatural lewdness. Transvestite.

Homosexuals (2x Greek) *Araenokoites:* a male engaging in same-gender sexual activity. Abuser of self with mankind. A sodomite.

Thieves (16x Greek) *Kleptes:* a thief who steals by stealth or in secret.

We have included here a key word study to expand the definitions of this unsavory list of sin, transgressions, and iniquities to be certain that people know what sin is. Our politically correct culture today is fulfilling the prophet Isaiah's words: Woe to those who call evil good, and good evil; who exchange darkness for light, and light for darkness; who exchange bitter for sweet, and sweet for bitter! Thus, many are confused and deceived about the Truth. Isaiah 5:20 MEV

In some local churches and in some entire Christian denominations today, there is little or no teaching about sin and we believe that at some level, part of the problem is many individuals today literally do not know what sinful behavior is according to the Word of God, not according to popular culture.

We have very clear instructions and commands here in the Scriptures that if an individual confessing Jesus Christ as the Lord of their life is openly living a lifestyle of sin, then we are to go in meekness, motivated by love for their soul, and help them see how they are wrong. Additionally, and anyone professing to be a Christian that is known to be guilty of one or more of these sins or iniquities, which means confirmation by witnesses (not gossip or rumor); then in obedience to God's Word we are to follow the incremental four step (hopefully step four is not required) process as commanded by Jesus:

Step #1: Go and meet privately with the offending brother/sister and tell them of the sin/offence. If there is no repentance and reconciliation, then we are to:

Step #2: Go and meet with the individual with one or two additional witnesses and seek their repentance. If there is still no sincere change of heart, we are:

Step #3: Then make the transgression known to the congregation, still hopeful that they will see their wrongdoing. But, if the offending person still will not acknowledge their sin and repent: Step #4: They should be asked to separate themselves from the local church fellowship.

Of course, this calls for much prayer and mature spiritual discernment; with the objective first and always being reconciliation of the relationship and restoration of all the individuals involved or adversely affected.

We should never approach any person before we have earnestly prayed and sought the guidance of the Holy Spirit. Another word of wisdom to carefully consider; if you really want to go and correct the offender, perhaps you should slow down and check your heart, your motives, and your humility first before you take any further action.

Brothers, if a man is caught in any transgression, you who are spiritual should restore such a one in a spirit of meekness, watching yourselves, lest you also be tempted. Galatians 6:1 MEV

Brothers, if any one of you strays from the truth and someone corrects him, let him know that he who converts the sinner from the error of his way will save a soul from death and will cover a multitude of sins. James 5:19 MEV

Now we exhort you, brothers, warn those who are unruly, comfort the faint-hearted, support the weak, be patient toward everyone. See that no one renders evil for evil to anyone. But always seek to do good to one another and to all. I Thessalonians 5:14-15 MEV

But, speaking the truth in love, may grow up in all things into Him, who is the head, Christ Himself, from whom the whole body is joined together and connected by every joint and ligament, as every part effectively does its work and grows, building itself up in love. Ephesians 4:15-16 MEV

The servant of the Lord must not quarrel, but must be gentle toward all people, able to teach, patient, in gentleness correcting those who are in opposition. Perhaps God will grant them repentance to know the truth, and they may escape from the snare of the devil, after being taken captured by him to do his will. II Timothy 2:24-26 MEV

For there are many disorderly and unruly men who are idle (vain, empty) and misleading talkers and self-deceivers and deceivers of others. [This is true] especially of those of the circumcision party [who have come over from Judaism]. Their mouths must be stopped, for they are mentally distressing and subverting whole families by teaching what they ought not to teach, for the purpose of getting base advantage and disreputable gain. One of their very own, said, Cretans are always liars, hurtful beasts, idle and lazy gluttons. And this account of them is [really] true, rebuke them sharply [deal sternly, even severely with them], so that they may be sound in the faith and free of error, [And may show their soundness by] ceasing to give attention to Jewish myths and fables or to rules [laid down] by [mere] men who reject and turn their backs on the Truth. To the pure [in heart and conscience] all things are pure, but to the defiled and corrupt and unbelieving nothing is pure; their very minds and consciences are defiled and polluted. They profess to know God [to recognize, perceive, and be acquainted with Him], but deny and disown and renounce Him by what they do; they are detestable and loathsome, unbelieving and disobedient and disloyal and rebellious, and [they are] unfit and worthless for good work (deed or enterprise) of any kind. Titus 1:10-16 AMPC

One of the significant problems in the Church today is that in some occurrences, it is the Senior leader of the local body or congregation; or one of the pastors or other lay-leaders in the church that is guilty of the unrepentant sinful behavior or transgression against a fellow believer.

When this is the case, many times the only recourse for the local church member is to quietly withdraw from this group or body of believers and prayerfully begin to seek, with the Lord's help; a new place to worship and serve.

We know this seems like such a distasteful option, but; sadly; sometimes, the one in authority is the one deceived and has drifted into sin. Or, in some situations the Head Pastor or the senior leadership simply refuse to recognize the problem behavior as defined in the Word of God; and they will not deal with the subordinate pastor/leader that is involved in the ungodly and destructive behavior, and thus they become a stumbling stone and are hurting others.

When this is the case, we must withdraw from this company of people and let the Lord Jesus deal with these blinded and corrupt leaders, just as He said He would in chapter two and three of the book of Revelation, in His letters to the churches.

Choosing to continue to attend and support such a church where the leadership is involved in sinful attitudes, behavior, or activities; or is turning a blind eye to the sin and iniquity of others in leadership positions within the local congregation, is a very serious matter. You must know that if you make the decision to do be a coward and do nothing, then you are guilty of enabling such behavior and have become complicit in the misconduct and a partaker in their evil.

When I say to the wicked, "O wicked man you shall surely die!" And you do not speak to warn the wicked from his way, that wicked man shall die in his iniquity. But his blood I will require from your hand. Nevertheless, if you warn the wicked to turn from his way and he does not turn from his way, he shall die in his iniquity. But you have been delivered your soul.
Ezekiel 33:8-9 MEV

Then Jesus came and spoke to them, saying, All authority has been given to Me in heaven and on earth. Go therefore and make disciples of all nations, baptizing them in the name of the Father and of the Son and of the Holy Spirit, teaching them to observe all things that I have commanded you. And remember, I am with you always, even to the end of the age. Amen.
Matthew 28:18-20 MEV

Therefore I testify to you this day that I am innocent of the blood of all men. For I did not keep from declaring to you the whole counsel of God. Therefore take heed of yourselves and to the entire flock, over which the Holy Spirit has made you overseers, to shepherd the church of God which He purchased with His own blood. Acts 20:26-28 MEV

Anyone who runs on ahead [of God] and does not abide in the doctrine of Christ [who is not content with what He taught] does not have God; but he who continues to live in the doctrine (teaching) of Christ [does have God], he has both the Father and the Son. If anyone comes to you and does not bring this doctrine [is disloyal to what Jesus Christ taught], do not receive him [do not accept him, do not welcome or admit him] into [your] house or bid him Godspeed or give him any encouragement. For he who wishes him success [who encourages him, wishing him Godspeed] is a partaker in his evil doings. II John 9-11 AMPC

We must remember that in the first century when this letter was composed by apostle John, the church members met house to house (Acts 2:46, 5:42, 12:12) because there were not designated buildings constructed for such gatherings of the congregation of Christ's followers until the third century AD. The first known building devoted to Christian gatherings and worship is at Dura Europos on the Euphrates river in eastern Syria, near the village of Salhiye on the border with Iraq. This was an existing house that was expanded to accommodate the larger and growing gatherings along with the other various church functions around 250 AD.

The agape love of God always does what is best for others, and agape love always speaks the Truth; and the Truth is the whole council of God, not just the portions we find pleasant and personally convenient.

Love does no harm to a neighbor; therefore love is the fulfilment of the law. Romans 13:10 MEV

When an individual that confesses to be a follower of Jesus Christ is guilty of committing a sin against another believer, then The Word is clear that we must go to that person and speak the Truth in love, with the goal always to be reconciliation, restoration, and maintaining unity within the body of Christ.

Have you ever pondered why there seems to be a growing sin problem in the church? And why it seems to be an increasingly common occurrence to hear about, yet another church leader involved in some ungodly behavior or unrepentant sinful lifestyle?

Well, at least part of the answer lies in the fact that this matter of church correction and discipline has been effectively ignored in many local congregations and denominations.

Proper Word-based correction and discipline is not being taught or practiced by many of the leaders of the various Bible believing Christian congregations that claim to adhere to all the teachings of Jesus Christ.

Iniquity and sin allows the devil an open door into our churches, homes, and our lives. This is one of the chief reasons why the Church is sick & weak, and not the salt & light we are called-out to be within our homes, communities, culture, and in our world today.

We must believe, obey, and practice the whole council of God. We can not pick and choose the precepts, commands, and doctrines that we like and ignore the others. In doing so, we are creating a Jesus in our image, not the other way around. We are called to love the Lord with our whole being, spirit, soul, and body; and He alone determines and defines what loving Him looks like, just as Jesus said:

If you love Me, keep My commandments. John 14:15 MEV

He who has My commandments and keeps them is the one who loves Me. And he who loves Me will be

The Believer's Mandate

loved by My Father. And I will love him and will reveal Myself to him. John 14:21 MEV

My little children, I am writhing these things to you, so that you do not sin. But if anyone does sin, we have an Advocate with the Father, Jesus Christ the Righteous One. He is the atoning sacrifice for our sins, and not only ours only, but also for the sins of the whole world. By this we know that we know Him, if we keep His commandments. I John 2:1-3 MEV

Why is sin perverting and defiling the camp? Because many pastors and Church leaders have compromised and have allowed it to persist, and these issues have not been dealt with as Jesus has commanded in His Word. We can only conclude that these individuals do not really understand what ultimately this continued rebellion will cost them in the age to come.

We must read, study, and obey the whole council of God, which is the Word of God; even the passages of Scripture we do not necessarily savor, or the Word that does not line-up with the widely held beliefs within our families, traditions, communities, and our culture at large.

This is the Believer's Mandate.

Chapter Eighteen

The American dream

F oundational Truth: If Jesus is not Lord of all, He is not Lord at all.

The *Merriam-Webster* definition of the American dream: A happy way of living that is thought of by many Americans as something that can be achieved by anyone in the United States especially by working hard and becoming successful; "With good jobs, a nice house, two children, and plenty of money, they believed they were living the American dream."

This dream has its origins rooted in the United States Declaration of Independence that was ratified July 4th, 1776 at Independence Hall in Philadelphia, Pennsylvania. And principally, the second paragraph of this foundational document is where this notion of the American dream springs forth in our thoughts. It reads thus:

We hold these truths to be self-evident, that all men are created equal, that they are endowed by their Creator with certain unalienable Rights, that among these are Life, Liberty and the pursuit of Happiness.

The United States of America was instituted as a Christian nation, and for compelling evidence of that indisputable fact one need not look any further than the official motto of this great Republic: "In God We Trust." We further believe that it is beyond dispute that these foundational principles crafted by our founding fathers were formed and modeled from the infallible Truths and precepts recorded in the Word of God.

However, we also believe there are some serious flaws and misconceptions in the commonly held view and subsequent definition of the American dream and bringing light and clarity to those flawed beliefs is the focus of this dissertation.

Of course, there are many secular world views that could be mentioned, but; we have no interest whatsoever in any non-biblical world view and will not be addressing any of those various opinions and theories because they are all based on varying degrees of deception propagated by satan, the god of this world and the enemy of our soul.

From this widely held belief in the so-called American dream tradition, many in the Church today have formed what we have characterized as the American gospel, and one can find the maxims of this American gospel recorded in the books in Christian book outlets and preached each week from the sermons of some of the most popular ministers and the very largest churches throughout America.

The premise of this teaching is not to criticize others, but; to apply Scriptural Truth to these widely held views of this contrived and Americanized gospel that are not rooted and grounded in the Word of God. We believe in the Truth and the original declaration of independence and liberty from the oppressive kingdom of this world and its evil ruler that in-fact holds so many in bondage as slaves.

Then Jesus said to those Jews who believed Him, If you remain in My word, then you are truly My disciples. You shall know the truth, and the truth shall set you free. John 8:31-32 MEV

When I was a young boy, my parents were killed, and I was adopted by a family in the Ozark Mountain country. Growing up on a small farm/ranch in a wilderness area in the center of the Bible belt of America was my beginning. As a teenager, I began to think about my future and plot my path to prosperity, so; I asked my father for advice and direction.

First, I suppose I should mention that we were Christians and we faithfully attended a small denominational country church out in the sticks. We were there every time the doors were open; Sunday morning, Sunday night, Wednesday evening and any other time there was special meeting or gathering. My entire world was the outdoors, ranch work, rural public school, and church activities, until I got old enough and big enough to work for hire.

My father has gone home to be with the Lord now, and I would never want to dishonor him in any way, but; his worldview was very typical of our area during the 1960's and 70's and was grounded in the American dream that is based on and filtered through the American gospel. Consequently, his advice about success in life was influenced as such. In my limited view of the world, my father was intelligent, hardworking, and honest. In summary, he was the smartest and wisest man I knew and he and the country denominational church we all attended taught me the American gospel.

So, what is this Americanized gospel and American dream?

The first and primary maxim of this Americanized gospel/dream worldview is this: You can become anything you want to become and do anything you want to do; if you will apply yourself and work hard enough, and long enough; and go to church when you can. Do this and you can and will achieve your goals.

This was "preached" to me for as far back as I have any memory of those days, and we heard repeatedly "You can be anything you want to be" if you work hard, stay out of trouble, and go to church. My level of success in life was totally up to me and my ability and my effort as I applied myself to obtaining my goal. Yes, we were taught you simply must want it bad enough.

Another saying that got drilled into my beliefs in my late teens was: Yes, these are the ten most important two-letter words in the English language: "If it is to be, it is up to me."

You can search the popular Christian book outlets in America and just explore the titles of the bestselling books and understand that this "self-help gospel" is alive and well in America.

You will see such titles as "Self Esteem: The New Reformation" or "The Power of Positive Thinking" or

"Self-Improvement 101" and many others like these, but; hopefully you get the idea. These books focus on you and how you are going to be improved and enhance your success and prosperity through your efforts. Nonetheless, this increasingly popular philosophy of self-ambition is a big problem in the Church today. This thinking is worldly and carnal.

We are not condemning these various books and their Authors, however; we are strongly suggesting that we must take all our thoughts, beliefs, and man-made traditions back to the plumb-line of our lives, which is the Word of God. What is our big problem here? Okay, we shall employ a prime example from our own life experiences, so we are not accused of picking on anyone else.

Have you ever heard something like this allegedly quoted from the Bible: "Don't you know brother that God helps those that help themselves?" Well, this is not in the Holy Bible and furthermore the Scriptures teach almost the exact opposite. (see Proverbs 28:26, Romans 2:8, Philippians 2:3-4)

Lean on, trust in, and be confident in the Lord with all your heart and mind and do not rely on your insight or understanding. In all your ways know, recognize, and acknowledge Him, and He will direct and make straight and plain your paths.

Proverbs 3:5-6 AMPC

Roll your works upon the Lord [commit and trust them wholly to Him; He will cause your thoughts to become agreeable to His will, and] so shall your plans be established and succeed. Proverbs 16:3 AMPC

If you are wise and understand God's ways, prove it by living an honorable life, doing good works with humility that comes from wisdom. But if you are bitterly jealous and there is selfish ambition in your heart, don't cover up the truth with boasting and lying. For jealously and selfishness are not God's kind of wisdom. Such things are earthly, unspiritual, and demonic. For wherever there is jealousy and selfish ambition, there you will find disorder and evil of every kind. James 3:13-16 NLT

We don't need more self-esteem, we need to know who we are in Christ. We don't need self-help, we need God's help. We don't need the power of positive thinking, we need the mind of Christ. We don't need life coaches, we need preachers and teachers submitted to Jesus Christ. We don't need drugs and therapy, we need to repent and obey the Truth.

The rudiments of these very popular self-help, "it's up to me" principles are not true. Yes, we state this again for absolute clarity; these widely held theories and maxims about success and prosperity in life are falsehoods, lies, and twisted half-truths at best. Yes, if we buy-in to this American dream concept; we have a big problem. These common-sensical sounding ideas simply do not line-up with the Word of God because they are the wisdom of this world and its system, which when practiced will position you at-odds with the doctrines that Jesus taught.

Whoa now, before you reach for a rock to throw at us, please stay engaged with us as we continue to examine this topic, nonetheless; we do intend to reveal and speak the Truth.

We want to be very clear here. We do not want to be critical of any group or anyone personally, except to say that many good-hearted people are deceived today, just as we once were.

By the grace of God, I got saved in that little county church, but; frankly I learned very little else about the Truths in the Word of God. Such basic Truths like how to study the Bible and how to become a real follower and true disciple of Jesus Christ. It wasn't until later in my faith journey in search of the Truth that I

The American Dream

discovered what real prosperity and success in this life is, and that was after working very hard in pursuit of my plans, goals, dreams, and selfish ambitions; and utterly failing. Thank God that I did crash and burn, or I might have never discovered the Truth.

Let's look at these popular carnal, worldly principles and see how they line-up with the Word of God.

Worldly precept: You can do anything that you want to do. No, that is not what Jesus taught.

Therefore Jesus answered and was saying to them, Truly, truly, I say to you, the Son can do nothing of Himself, but what He sees the Father do. For whatever He does, likewise the Son does. John 5:19 MEV

I can do nothing of Myself. As I hear, I judge. My judgement is just, because I seek not My own will, but the will of the Father who sent Me. John 5:30 MEV

For I came down from heaven, not to do My own will, but the will of Him who sent Me. John 6:38 MEV

As You sent Me into the world, so I sent them into the world. John 17:18 MEV

So Jesus said to them again, Peace be with you. as My Father has sent Me, even so I send you. John 20:21 MEV

Jesus said He could not do anything on His own because He was sent by the Father to only do the will of the Father (Luke 22:42) in total submission and obedience.

We are called to be just like Jesus in every way (II Corinthians 3:18), and Jesus clearly said that we are being sent by Him into the world exactly the same way that Jesus was sent by His Father. We are not here to do our will or fulfill our plans, but to do the will of our Lord in total submission and obedience to the Word.

Worldly precept: You can be anything you want to be. No, that is not what Jesus taught.

Then He said to them all, If anyone will come after Me, let him deny himself, and take up his cross daily, and follow Me. For whoever will save his life will lose it, but whoever loses his life for My sake will save it. For what does it profit a man if he gains the whole world, yet loses or forfeits himself? Luke 9:23-25 MEV

Large crowds went with Him. And He turned and said to them, If anyone comes to Me and does not hate his father and mother and wife and children and brothers and sisters, yes, and even his own life, he cannot be My disciple. And whoever does not bear his cross and follow Me cannot be My disciple.

For who among you, intending to build a tower, does not sit down first and count the cost to see whether he has resources to complete it? Otherwise, perhaps, after he has laid a foundation and is not able to complete it, all who see it begin to mock him, saying, This man began to build and was not able to complete it. Or what king, going to wage war against another king, does not sit down first and take counsel whether he is able with ten thousand to meet him who comes against him with twenty thousand? Otherwise, while the other is yet at a distance, he sends a delegation and requests conditions of peace. So likewise, any of you who does not forsake all that he has cannot be My disciple. Luke 14:25-33 MEV

Jesus has clearly commanded us that we are to deny ourselves which means we are to lay down and yield our plans, hopes, and dreams and to seek out and discover the plans and purposes that He has for our lives. We are to realize that this truly means everything in our lives, including all our family. We are to carefully consider and know that this will potentially cause stress and difficulty, but; that is not a justification for not following Him. No, we cannot be anything we want to be because that would make you and me the lord of our life, not Jesus.

Worldly precept: If it is to be, it is up to me. No, this is not what Jesus taught.

The Believer's Mandate

I am the true vine, and My Father is the vinedresser. Every branch in Me that bears no fruit, He takes away. And every branch that bears fruit, He prunes, that it may bear more fruit. You are already clean through the word which I have spoken to you. Remain in Me, as I also remain in you. As the branch cannot bear fruit by itself, unless it remains in the vine, neither can you, unless you remain in Me. I am the vine, you are the branches. He who remains in Me, and I in him, bears much fruit. For without Me you can do nothing. If a man does not remain in Me, he is thrown out as a branch and withers. And they gather them and throw them into the fire, and they are burned. If you remain in Me, and My words remain in you, you will ask whatever you desire, and it shall be done for you. My Father is glorified by this, that you bear much fruit; so you will be My disciples. John 15:1-8 MEV

If it is to be, it shall be up to Jesus Christ, the Master and Creator of the universe (Colossians 1:13-20) not you or me. Jesus said that apart from Him you and I can do nothing.

Of course, we could do lots of things in our own selfish ambition and desires, but; those things will have absolutely no eternal value and will only benefit the kingdom of darkness and the god of this world.

The American Dream

This naïve idea that Jesus came to this earth to be beaten, whipped, humiliated, tortured, crucified, and descend into hell, and then to be raised from the dead and ascend on high, just so you could live a happy life with plenty of money is not true. First of all, happiness is an emotion, and like all emotions they are unstable and subject to change depending on many external factors and circumstances in our earthly lives.

No, Jesus came into this world and allowed Himself to be crucified so that you and I could be reconciled back to the Father (I Peter 3:18) and to give us a living hope and a future inheritance in heaven with Him (I Peter 1:3-5).

What Jesus did promise His faithful followers is that He would never leave us or forsake us (Hebrews 13:5-6), no matter what the storms of life might bring. We can have an abundant and overflowing life in Him (John 10:10) despite our enemies' best efforts, if we choose to build our lives on the Rock (Matthew 7:24-27) and stand firm in our faith in Him (I Corinthians 15:57-58). Always abounding in our work for the Lord, knowing our toil is not in vain in the Lord.

Jesus is the vine and life-source and as we stay connected to that life-giving vine, we shall bear much fruit. This fruit is the fruit of the Spirit: Love, joy, peace, patience, kindness, goodness, faithfulness, gentleness, and self-control (Galatians 5:22-23). This is the fruit that glorifies the Father and remains forevermore, and proves we are true disciples of our Savior and Lord, Jesus.

No, the so-called and contrived American dream is not from our heavenly Father and does not and will not provide the things we need to truly prosper in this world, or the kingdom age to come. Jesus has very succinctly commanded us what we must do, and then we shall receive everything we need in this life.

But seek first the kingdom of God and His righteousness, and all these things shall be given to you. Matthew 6:33 MEV

We must first seek King Jesus and His domain and His way of doing things. When we choose to do life His way, not the worlds way; He has promised to fully supply everything that we need to prosper in this lifetime, and to receive our vast inheritance for all eternity.

Look, I am coming soon! My reward is with Me to give to each one according to his work. I am the Alpha and the Omega, the Beginning and the End, the First and the Last. Blessed are those who do His commandments, that they may have the right to the tree of life, and may enter through the gates into the city. Revelation 22:12-14 MEV

Jesus is the Aleph and the Tav, the Alpha and the Omega, the First and the Last, the Beginning and the End. We must accept Jesus as the Savior of our past and present; and surrender completely to Him as the Lord of our future life here on earth and the kingdom age to come.

This is the Believer's Mandate.

Chapter Nineteen

How to receive God's blessings

F oundational Truth: God Almighty is not moved by need - He is moved by faith.

If we were able to survey believers around the world, we believe this question would no doubt be in everyone's top ten list of inquiries that they would desperately desire a clear answer to. The objective of this teaching is to help answer this awesome question. How do I receive the promised blessings of God into my life?

The answer to this question and all of life's questions and requests come from one source, which is the book of Truth, the Holy Bible.

Background and context:

How To Receive God's Blessings

The Torah required each adult male (twenty years old and above) to present himself before the Lord with an offering, three times each year in Jerusalem, for the Feast of Unleavened Bread (Passover), the Feast of Weeks (Pentecost), and the Feast of Tabernacles. (Deuteronomy 16:16-17)

The time frame and setting of this teaching is approximately eight to ten days before Jesus' crucifixion, as He and His disciples were traveling to Jerusalem for the Feast of Passover, *the real Passover*.

There were basically two well established North-South routes from the Galilee area to Jerusalem. The first was the most direct route which went right through the middle of Samaria, and the second route was a bit longer, but; it was east of the Jordan river and avoided traveling through Samaria. This is the route Jesus took on His final journey (Matthew 19:1). This trail came south through Perea to the ford where Joshua crossed the Jordan river, then continued approximately six miles across the valley to Jericho. The city of Jericho is eight hundred feet below sea level and Jerusalem is about two thousand five hundred feet above sea level. (Elevation differential = 3300 feet).

Jericho means "City of the moon" (because it was known for its moon worshippers) and it is the oldest continually occupied city in the world. Jericho is called the 'City of Palms' (Deuteronomy 34:3) and it was the location of Elisha's healed spring (II Kings 2:19-22). Jericho was an oasis in the desert and a winter resort for the rich and famous, and as such; king Herod had his winter palace in Jericho. The City was also the home of twelve thousand priests and Levites at the beginning of the first century AD.

Jericho prophetically represents the world system, or man's government just as Jerusalem represents God's government. There is much that could be said about Jericho, but; for this particular teaching, we shall move along.

The road between Jericho up to Jerusalem was approximately eighteen miles and was full of switch-backs as one ascended the more than two-thirds of a mile in elevation, and would have been a day's journey walking, so; Jesus and His followers would have stopped in Jericho to lodge for the night before their full day hike up to the city of Jerusalem the next day.

Entering the city of Jericho:

We see recorded in the Gospel of Luke Jesus and His disciples accompanied by a great crowd; were approaching Jericho from the east after crossing the Jordan river, that Jesus encounters and brings healing to the first nameless blind man outside the City gates (Luke 18:35-43).

Once the multitude had entered the City gates, then we see Jesus encountering the chief tax collector, Zacchaeus; with whom Jesus lodged for the night and changed Zacchaeus's (which means Justified) life forever (Luke 19:1-10).

The next day Jesus continued His travel towards Jerusalem and encounters two more anonymous blind men (Matthew 20:29-34), and after laying His hands on them and restoring their sight, Jesus continues His journey away from City; at which He encounters yet another man with a disease that has caused his blindness. Please turn to the Gospel of Mark chapter 10:46-52, and we shall take a closer look at this significant Jesus encounter.

Exiting the city of Jericho:

As Jesus and His disciples walked out of town surrounded by a huge crowd of people, there sat a man beside the roadway begging for a pittance. First, we need to understand that there is no Hebrew word for a professional "beggar" in the Scriptures, but; there is clear instruction in the Torah commanding that the poor, the stranger, the fatherless, and the widow be cared for (Exodus 22:21-27, Leviticus 19:10, Deuteronomy

24:17-22, Deuteronomy 26:12). So, if everyone was obedient to the Word of God, there would not be any blind beggar's.

During the first century *Anno Domini*, the destitute among the people would wear an outer garment that everyone identified as a beggar's garment or cloak. This mantle became the infirmed vagabonds "license" to set out in the public view and solicit for handouts. The fact that there are several accounts of beggars in the New Testament (Luke 16:20, John 9:8, Acts 3:2) is yet another witness to the fact that the Jewish leadership were morally backslidden and had just become religious practitioners of the law for their own prestige. (Luke 14:13, James 1:27, James 2:8)

Then they came to Jericho. And as He went out of Jericho with His disciples and a great number of people, blind Bartimaeus, the son of Timaeus, sat along the way begging. Mark 10:46 MEV

Why would the Holy Spirit tell us that *Bartimaeus* – the *son of Timaeus* sat beside the road begging? *Bar* is the Aramaic word for son. So; to call this blind man *Bartimaeus* is to call him *son of Timaeus*. What then, is the Holy Spirit wanting us to know?

Timaeus in Aramaic means Uncleanness, so; Bartimaeus means "Son of uncleanness" which tells us that Bartimaeus was blinded by a contagious eye disease, which would make him a legal and social outcast, and no one would want to come near him physically.

We have studied various encyclopedias and historical accounts of the lifestyles of the people and Middle Eastern culture to glean understanding of the eastern mindset and their routines. One of the areas that we have considered is the various plagues and diseases. One very common infectious disease during the first century was Egyptian Ophthalmia or better known as *Trachoma*.

This disease was commonly spread by flies and was contracted most often in children. This pestilence is still a problem in the impoverished areas in Asia, Africa, and the Middle East today. This bacterial disease untreated led to total blindness. We have read estimates that as much as 20% of the population suffered from this and other blinding diseases during the first century AD.

The historian Josephus in *The Wars of the Jews* – (Book 6/Chapter 9) estimated the population of Judah and Jerusalem during the Passover Feast, totaling between two million five hundred thousand and three million adults during the Feast days, based on the number of sacrifices at the Temple. If we took the conservative estimate and just assumed half of the estimated infectious rate, it still amounts to more than two hundred fifty thousand blind adults in Judah and Jerusalem. Wow, this was a substantial civil problem.

Now, back to the Scriptures in Mark chapter ten.

When he heard that it was Jesus of Nazareth, he began to cry out, Jesus, Son of David, have mercy on me! Mark 10:47 MEV

Many ordered him to keep silent. But he cried out even more, Son of David, have mercy on me! Mark 10:48 MEV

Why was this blind man crying out "Son of David" when they had just told him it was Jesus of Nazareth? And why would he be so desperately asking for mercy from this man walking by?

The Greek word *Eleeo*, which is translated to the English word mercy; means covenant-loyalty.

Also, take note of the fact that those that were in front of Jesus were telling this blind man to shut-up and keep silent. Big lesson here: Don't get out in front of Jesus. We are supposed to follow Him.

Jesus stood still and commanded him to be called. So they called the blind man, saying, Be of good comfort. Rise, He is calling you. Mark 10:49 MEV

Okay, can you see this blind beggar sitting on the roadside, with his outer garment spread-out about him so he could capture the alms and offerings that those passing by might throw his way. People would not have wanted to come very close for fear they might catch his dreadful disease. However; Bartimaeus hears a commotion and knows instinctively someone important must be passing through. He overhears somebody say it was this Jesus from Nazareth that had everyone in Judea stirred-up, and something happens. What happens?

Faith exploded in this man's heart, and faith is the conduit to the promises and blessings of God!

Throwing aside his garment, he rose and came to Jesus. Mark 10:50 MEV

This man threw aside his outer garment. The garment that was his shelter from the elements, and his identity, and his way of making a living, and he threw it aside, Glory to God. This is faith because faith is an act.

Jesus answered him, What do you want Me to do for you? Mark 10:51a MEV

Jesus answered him? What exactly was Jesus answering?

Jesus was answering this man's heart cry of faith "Son of David, have mercy on me," or in other words he was declaring; "You are the Messiah, and I am in covenant with you."

What precisely do you think this blind man believed? He believed the prophecies in the Word of God about the promised Messiah. II Samuel 7:12-13, Psalm 132:11-12, Isaiah 9:6-7, Isaiah 35:5, Isaiah 42:7, Isaiah 61:1, and Jesus of Nazareth's testimony written in Luke 4:16-21.

The blind man said to Him, Rabbi, that I might receive my sight. Mark 10:51b MEV

Jesus said to him, Go your way. Your faith has made you well. Immediately he received his sight and followed Jesus on the way. Mark 10:52 MEV

Glory to God, hallelujah! What caused this man to be healed?

His Faith! Faith in what? He heard the Word and believed in his heart!

Here in this passage of Scripture is the answer to our question of how we receive all of Father God's blessings into our lives: By our faith in His Word.

You **hear** the Word.
You **believe** the Word.
You **act** on the Word.
You **receive** from the Word.

This is faith, and our faith is how we receive everything from our Lord.

Blind Bartimaeus did not own a Bible because there wasn't any. Bartimaeus obviously didn't read the Scriptures because he was blind. Bartimaeus was not born-again or spirit-filled, but; he was in blood covenant with God, which we call the Old Covenant.

Blind Bartimaeus heard the Word and meditated on that Word long enough that he believed the Word in his heart. When he heard the promised Messiah, who was the Son of David coming by; he acted on his faith in the Word that he believed to be the Truth and began to shout and would not shut-up until Jesus stopped and called for him. When Bartimaeus arose, and cast away his beggar's cloak, God Almighty took notice from heaven, and Bartimaeus received exactly what he was believing for, his sight! Glory to God, thank you Jesus.

God is not moved by need, He is moved by faith.

Bartimaeus and three other blind men all received their sight outside the gates of Jericho those days, and every one of those men received their miracle provision exactly the very same way, by their faith in the Word of God and under the Old Covenant.

But as born-again believer's in Jesus Christ, (Hebrews 8:6) we are under a New Covenant which is established on even better promises!

Now, we search the Scriptures and find the promise in God's Word that answers our problem, and we read the Word and speak the Word and meditate on the Word long enough for us to get the revelation of that Truth in our spirit, and then we patiently wait for the manifestation of that promise in our life. We receive salvation, deliverance, provision, guidance, protection, comfort, peace, and healing exactly the very same way, by our faith in the Word of God.

If you are a born-again child of God, then by faith, you shall receive just what you are believing for, in the name of Jesus Christ. Again, how do we receive blessings from God?

> We **hear** the Word.
> We **believe** the Word.
> We **act** on the Word.
> We **receive** the promise in the Word.
> Amen.

The clarion call. Why are we here on this planet?

We are all here by the grace of Almighty God to fulfill the mandate given to us by the One who gave it all, Jesus Christ of Nazareth. We are to hear and believe the Good news that Jesus, the Son of the living God; came here to earth to pay the ransom for our redemption, so we can be saved out from the kingdom of darkness and eternal death and to be translated into the kingdom of light and eternal life, however; we all must choose Jesus as our Savior and Lord.

This is the first step for everyone, so; just as the Word of God says in Romans 10:9-10,13: that if you confess with your mouth Jesus is Lord, and believe in your heart that God has raised Him from the dead, you will be saved, for with the heart one believes unto righteousness, and with the mouth confession is made unto salvation. For, "Everyone who calls on the name of the Lord shall be saved."

Jesus the Son of David is passing by right now. Will you cry out to Him now? This is the will of the Father, however; we all must choose Him.

This is the Believer's Mandate.

∼∼∼

In every human being's life, these words will be spoken: "Thy will be done."

And either you will say it, or at the end of your life here on earth, God will say it.

Selah

CHAPTER TWENTY

The Name above all names

There are many types, shadows, similitudes, and names of God in the Holy Scriptures. All of these taken together provide a progressive revelation of our heavenly Father's character as the Holy Spirit, who Authored the Scriptures; moved on faithful men to transcribe God's word for all future generations to study. However; because of Jesus' absolute humble obedience, great love, and sacrifice; God Almighty has declared that there is **One Name** that is so much greater than every other name that we are commanded to exalt, magnify, and honor that name above all other names, and this is our humble attempt to magnify that Name.

I love You, Oh Lord, my strength. Psalm 18:1 MEV

The Name Above All Names

Let this mind be in you all, which was also in Christ Jesus, who, being in the form of God, did not consider equality with God something to be grasped. But He emptied Himself, taking upon Himself the form of a servant, and was made in the likeness of men. And being found in the form of a man, He humbled Himself and became obedient to death, even death on a cross. Therefore God highly exalted Him, and gave Him the name which is above every name, that at the name of Jesus every knee should bow, of those in heaven and on earth and under the earth, and every tongue should confess that Jesus Christ is Lord, to the glory of God the Father. Philippians 2:5-11 MEV

There is no salvation in any other, for there is no other name under heaven given among men by which we must be saved. Acts 4:12 MEV

This is the word of faith that we preach: that if you confess with your mouth Jesus is Lord, and believe in your heart that God has raised Him from the dead, you will be saved, for with the heart one believes unto righteousness, and with the mouth confession is made unto salvation. For the Scripture says, Whoever believes in Him will not be ashamed. For there is no distinction between Jew and Greek, for the same Lord over all is generous toward all who call upon Him. For,

The Believer's Mandate

Everyone who calls on the name of the Lord shall be saved. Romans 10:8b-13 MEV

Following is a listing of more than three hundred fifty names and titles for Jesus organized in alphabetical order. We do not represent this labor of love as an exhaustive or complete list, however; it is a good start to assist your own personal search of the Scriptures to discover the manifold grace of our Lord Jesus Christ throughout the Bible, and ultimately develop your confidence in God's Word. Faith comes when the will of God is known, and through the names, titles, and similitudes of Jesus, the will of the Father shall be revealed to us all through His Beloved Son. Amen.

He who sees Me sees Him who sent Me. John 12:45 MEV

Advocate (I John 2:1) **Almighty** (Revelation 1:8) **Alpha and the Omega** (Revelation 1:8) **Amen** (Revelation 3:14) **Anchor of the soul** (Hebrews 6:19) **Ancient of Days** (Daniel 7:22) **Angel of His Presence** (Isaiah 63:9) **Anointed** (Psalm 2:2) **Apostle** (Hebrews 3:1) **Apple Tree** (Song of Songs 2:3) **Appointed Heir of all things** (Hebrews 1:2) **Ark of the Covenant** (Hebrews 9:4) **Attested by God** (Acts 2:22) **Atoning Sacrifice for our sins** (I John

2:2) **Author and Finisher of our faith** (Hebrews 12:2) **Author of their salvation** (Hebrews 2:10)

Baby (Luke 2:12) **Baptizer with the Holy Spirit and with fire** (Luke 3:16) **Banner to the peoples** (Isaiah 11:10) **Beginning of the creation of God** (Revelation 3:14) **Beginning and the End** (Revelation 21:6) **Bethel** (Genesis 28:19) **Blessed and only Ruler** (I Timothy 6:15) **Branch** (Isaiah 11:1) **Bread of God** (John 6:33) **Bread of Life** (John 6:35) **Bridegroom** (John 3:29) **Bright and Morning Star** (Revelation 22:16) **Brightness of His glory** (Hebrews 1:3) **Bronze serpent on a pole** (Numbers 21:9) **Builder of the Church** (Matthew 16:18) **Bundle of Myrrh** (Song of Songs 1:13)

Carpenter's Son (Matthew 13:55) **Chief Cornerstone** (Ephesians 2:20) **Chief Shepherd** (I Peter 5:4) **Child** (Luke 2:40) **Child Jesus** (Luke 2:27) **Chosen One of God** (Luke 23:35) **Christ of God** (Luke 9:20) **Christ Jesus my Lord** (Philippians 3:8) **Christ the Lord** (Luke 2:11) **Cluster of henna blossoms** (Song of Songs 1:14) **Commanded Blessing** (Deuteronomy 28:8) **Consolation of Israel** (Luke 2:25) **Counselor** (Isaiah 9:6) **Covenant of the people** (Isaiah 42:6) **Creator of Israel** (Isaiah 43:15) **Creator of Life** (Acts 3:15)

Deliverer (Psalm 18:2) **Deliverance** (Obadiah 1:17) **Destroyer of the works of the devil** (I John 3:8) **Distinguished among ten thousand** (Song of Songs 5:10) **Door** (John 10:9)

End of the Law (Romans 10:4) **Eternal Father** (Isaiah 9:6) **Eternal King** (I Timothy 1:17) **Eternal Life** (I John 5:20) **Everlasting High Priest** (Hebrews 6:20) **Everlasting Rock** (Isaiah 26:4) **Exceedingly great Reward** (Genesis 15:1) **Express Image of Himself** (Hebrews 1:3)

Faithful and True (Revelation 19:11) **Faithful and True Witness** (Revelation 3:14) **Faithful Witness** (Revelation 1:5) **Firstborn** (Romans 8:29) **Firstborn from the dead** (Revelation 1:5) **Firstborn of every creature** (Colossians 1:15) **First and the Last** (Revelation 1:17) **First fruits** (I Corinthians 15:20) **Foreigner in Jerusalem** (Luke 24:18) **Forerunner** (Hebrews 6:20) **Fortress** (II Samuel 22:2) **Foundation** (I Corinthians 3:11) **Fountain of living waters** (Jeremiah 2:13) **Fourth Man in the fire** (Daniel 3:25) **Friend of tax collectors and sinners** (Luke 7:34) **Friend who sticks closer than a brother** (Proverbs 18:24) **Fruit of the womb** (Luke 1:42) **Fulfillment of the Law** (Matthew 5:17) **Fuller's Soap** (Malachi 3:2)

Galilean (Luke 23:6) **Gate of heaven** (Genesis 28:17) **Gazelle or a Young Stag** (Song of Songs 2:9) **Glory of Your people Israel** (Luke 2:32) **God of the whole earth** (Isaiah 54:5) **Godhead** (Colossians 2:9) **Godly One** (Psalm 16:10) **Good Shepherd** (John 10:11) **Good Teacher** (Mark 10:17) **Governor** (Matthew 2:6) Grain of wheat (John 12:24) **Great God** (Jeremiah 32:18) **Great God and Savior Jesus Christ** (Titus 2:13) **Great Shepherd of the sheep** (Hebrews 13:20) **Greater than Solomon** (Matthew 12:42) **Guarantor of a better covenant** (Hebrews 7:22) **Guide** (Psalm 48:14)

Head of all authority and power (Colossians 2:10) **Head of every man** (I Corinthians 11:3) **Head of the body, the church** (Colossians 1:18) **Head and Savior of the church** (Ephesians 5:23) **Healer** (Matthew 14:14) **Heir of all things** (Hebrews 1:2) **Helper** (Hebrews 13:6) **Her Offspring** (Genesis 3:15) **Hiding Place** (Isaiah 32:2) **High Priest** (Hebrews 3:1) **High Priest over the house of God** (Hebrews 10:21) **Higher than the heavens** (Hebrews 7:26) **High Tower** (Psalm 18:2) **Highway of Holiness** (Isaiah 35:8) **Holy Son Jesus** (Acts 4:30) **Holy One** (Isaiah 43:15) **Holy One of Israel** (Isaiah 41:14) **Holy One of God** (Mark 1:24) **Holy and Righteous**

One (Acts 3:14) **Horn of Salvation** (Luke 1:69) **Horn of my Salvation** (Psalm 18:2) **Husband** (Isaiah 54:5) **Humble King** (Zechariah 9:9)

I AM (John 8:58) **I am alive forevermore** (Revelation 1:18) **I am a Worm, and not a man** (Psalm 22:6) **I am the Lord who heals you** (Exodus 15:26) **Image of the invisible God** (Colossians 1:15) **Immanuel** (Isaiah 7:14) **Immortal King** (I Timothy 1:17) **Intercessor** (Hebrews 7:25) **Invisible King** (I Timothy 1:17) **Its lamp is the Lamb** (Revelation 21:22)

Jesus (Matthew 1:21) **Jesus Christ** (Romans 1:6) **Jesus Christ our Lord** (Roman 1:3) **Jesus is the Lord** (I Corinthians 12:3) **Jesus Christ our Savior** (Titus 3:6) **Jesus of Nazareth** (Luke 4:34) **Jesus the Son of God** (Hebrews 4:14) **Jew** (John 4:9) **Judge of the living and the dead** (Acts 10:42) **Judge of Israel** (Micah 5:1) **Justifier** (Romans 3:26)

King (Matthew 21:5) **King of Glory** (Psalm 24:10) **King of Israel** (John 1:49) **King of kings** (Revelation 19:16) **King of saints** (Revelation 15:3) **King of the Jews** (John 19:19)

Ladder to heaven (Genesis 28:12, John 1:51) **Lamb** (Revelation 5:6) **Lamb of God** (John 1:29) **Lamb slain** (Revelation 13:8) **Lamb without**

blemish and without spot (I Peter 1:19) **Last Adam** (I Corinthians 15:45) **Lawgiver** (James 4:12) **Leader and Commander to the people** (Isaiah 55:4) **Life** (John 11:25) **Life-giving Spirit** (I Corinthians 15:45) **Light** (John 1:6) **Light of mankind** (John 1:4) **Light of the Gentiles** (Acts 13:47) **Light of the nations** (Isaiah 42:6) **Light for revelation to the Gentiles** (Luke 2:32) **Light of the world** (John 8:12) **Lily of the valleys** (Song of Songs 2:1) **Lion of the tribe of Judah** (Revelation 5:5) **Living Bread** (John 6:51) **Living Stone** (I Peter 2:4) **Lord** (Acts 1:6) **Lord of all** (Acts 10:36) **Lord and my God** (John 20:28) **Lord's Christ** (Luke 2:26) **Lord and Christ** (Acts 2:36) **Lord from heaven** (I Corinthians 15:47) **Lord God Almighty** (Revelation 15:3) **Lord of both the dead and the living** (Romans 14:9) **Lord of Hosts** (Psalm 24:10) **Lord of lords** (Revelation 17:14) **Lord our Righteousness** (Jeremiah 33:16) **Lord of the Harvest** (Luke 10:2) **Lord even of the Sabbath** (Mark 2:28) **Love** (I John 4:16)

Maker (Isaiah 54:5) **Man of sorrows** (Isaiah 53:3) **Master in heaven** (Colossians 4:1) **Mediator** (I Timothy 2:5) **Merciful and faithful High Priest** (Hebrews 2:17) **Messenger of the covenant** (Malachi 3:1) **Messiah** (Daniel 9:25) **Mighty God** (Isaiah

9:6) **Mighty One, Who will save** (Zephaniah 3:17) **Minister in the sanctuary and the true tabernacle** (Hebrews 8:2) **My Beloved** (Song of Songs 2:10) **MY Beloved Son** (Luke 3:22) **My Brother** (John 20:17) **MY Chosen One** (Isaiah 42:1) **My Confidence** (Psalm 71:5) **MY Covenant** (Genesis 6:18) **My Deliverer** (Psalm 18:2) **My Fortress** (Psalm 18:2) **My God** (Psalm 18:2) **My Help** (Psalm 70:5) **My Hope** (Psalm 71:5) **My Light** (Psalm 27:1) **My Lord** (Genesis 18:3) **My Pillar** (Psalm 18:2) **MY Servant** (Isaiah 42:1) **My High Tower** (Psalm 18:2) **My Redeemer lives** (Job 19:25) **My Rock** (Psalm 18:2) **My Salvation** (Psalm 27:1) **My Shepherd** (Psalm 23:1) **My Shield** (Psalm 18:2) **My Strength and my Song** (Psalm 118:14) **My Stronghold** (Psalm 71:3) **My Strong Refuge** (Psalm 71:7)

Nail in a firm place (Isaiah 22:23) **Name which is above every name** (Philippians 2:9) **Nazarene** (Matthew 2:23) **Neighbor** (Luke 10:36) **New and Living Way** (Hebrews 10:20)

Offering and a Sacrifice to God (Ephesians 5:2) **Offspring of David** (Revelation 22:16) **Omnipotent** (Revelation 19:6) **One Shepherd** (John 10:16) **One who raises up my head** (Psalm 3:3) **Only begotten Son** (John 3:16) **Only Son of the Father** (John

1:14) **Only Wise God** (I Timothy 1:17) **Ordained by God** (Acts 10:42) **Our Peace** (Ephesians 2:14) **Overcomer** (Revelation 17:14)

Passover (I Corinthians 5:7) **Perfect forever** (Hebrews 7:28) **Potter** (Romans 9:21) **Powerful in deed and Word** (Luke 24:19) **Power of God** (I Corinthians 1:24) **Preacher** (Luke 4:43) **Precious** (I Peter 2:7) **Precious Cornerstone** (Isaiah 28:16) **Priest** (Psalm 110:4) **Prince** (Daniel 9:25) **Prince of Peace** (Isaiah 9:6) **Prophet** (Deuteronomy 18:15) **Prophet from Nazareth** (Matthew 21:11)

Rabbi (John 1:38) **Ransom for all** (I Timothy 2:6) **Reconciler** (II Corinthians 5:19) **Redeemer** (Isaiah 41:14) **Redeeming Kinsman** (Ruth 3:9) **Refiner's Fire** (Malachi 3:2) **Refiner and Purifier of gold and silver** (Malachi 3:3) **Refuge from the storm** (Isaiah 25:4) **Repairer of the Breach** (Isaiah 58:12) **Restorer of Paths** (Isaiah 58:12) **Restores my soul** (Psalm 23:3) **Resurrection** (John 11:25) **Rewarder** (Hebrews 11:6) **Righteous Branch** (Jeremiah 23:5) **Righteous Man** (Luke 23:47) **Righteous One** (I John 2:1) **Righteous Servant** (Isaiah 53:11) **Rivers of water in a dry place** (Isaiah 32:2) **Rock** (I Corinthians 10:4) **Rock of Offence** (I Peter 2:8) **Root of David** (Revelation 5:5) **Root of Jesse** (Isaiah 11:10) **Root**

out of a dry ground (Isaiah 53:2) **Rose of Sharon** (Song of Songs 2:1) **Ruler** (Micah 5:2) **Ruler of the kings of the earth** (Revelation 1:5)

Salvation (Luke 2:30) **Samaritan** (Luke 10:33) **Savior** (Acts 5:31) **Savior of the world** (John 4:42) **Scepter shall not depart from Judah** (Genesis 49:10) **Scepter will rise out of Israel** (Numbers 24:17) **Second Man** (I Corinthians 15:47) **Seed of Abraham** (Galatians 3:16) **Servant** (Isaiah 42:1) **Shadow from the heat** (Isaiah 25:4) **Shelter from the tempest** (Isaiah 32:2) **Shepherd and Guardian of your souls** (I Peter 2:25) **Shield** (Genesis 15:1) **Shiloh** (Genesis 49:10) **Shoot from the stump of Jesse** (Isaiah 11:1) **Smoking Fire Pot with a Flaming Torch** (Genesis 15:17) **Son of Abraham** (Matthew 1:1) **Son of David** (Mark 10:47) **Son of God** (Mark 1:1) **Son of the Highest** (Luke 1:32) **Son of Joseph** (John 6:42) **Son of Man** (Luke 19:10) **Son of the Blessed One** (Mark 14:61) **Son of the Living God** (Matthew 16:16) **Source of eternal Salvation** (Hebrews 5:9) **Spring opened up** (Zechariah 13:1) **Stability of your times** (Isaiah 33:6) **Star will come out of Jacob** (Numbers 24:17) **Stone** (Isaiah 28:16) **Stone was cut out without hands** (Daniel 2:34) **Stone of stumbling** (I Peter 2:8) **Strength of my**

life (Psalm 27:1) **Stronghold in the day of distress** (Nahum 1:7) **Sun of Righteousness** (Malachi 4:2)

Teacher who has come from God (John 3:2) **Tender plant** (Isaiah 53:2) **Testator** (Hebrews 9:16) **Tested Stone** (Isaiah 28:16) **The Ark** (Genesis 7:1) **The Ark of the Testimony** (Exodus 25:22) **The Blessing** (Numbers 6:22) **The Christ** (Mark 14:61) **The Glory of the Lord** (Ezekiel 1:28) **The Life** (John 14:6) **The Lord** (Genesis 18:1) **The Lord Will Provide** (Genesis 22:14) **The Man** (John 19:6) **The Man Christ Jesus** (I Timothy 2:5) **The only Wise God our Savior** (Jude 1:24) **The Pillar of Cloud by day or the Pillar of Fire by night** (Exodus 13:22) **The same yesterday, and today, and forever** (Hebrews 13:8) **The Sign of the prophet Jonah** (Matthew 12:39-40) **The Sound** (Genesis 3:8) **The Truth** (John 14:6) **The Veil** (Hebrews 10:20) **The Way** (John 14:6) **The Word** (John 1:1) **Treasures of Wisdom and Knowledge** (Colossians 2:3) **Tree of Life** (Genesis 2:9) **True God** (I John 5:20) **True Vine** (John 15:1) **Temple in the city** (Revelation 21:22)

Vindicator (Isaiah 54:17)

Water of Life (Revelation 22:1) **Wealth of Salvation, Wisdom, and Knowledge** (Isaiah 33:6) **Who is and Who was and Who is to come**

(Revelation 1:8) **Why do you ask My name? It is too Wonderful** (Judges 13:18) **Wisdom of God** (I Corinthians 1:24) **Word of God** (Revelation 19:13) **Wonderful Counselor** (Isaiah 9:6)

You are a Samaritan (John 8:48) **Young Child** (Matthew 2:11) **Your King** (Isaiah 43:15) **Your Offspring** (Genesis 3:15) **Your Salvation** (Genesis 49:18) **Your Voice** (Genesis 3:10)

He who testifies to these things says, *Surely I am coming soon.* Amen. Even so, come Lord Jesus! The grace of our Lord Jesus Christ be with you all. Amen.

Revelation 22:20-21 MEV

Jesus is our soon coming King!

THE END *of the age is near.*

What's next: The Kingdom age.

CPSIA information can be obtained
at www.ICGtesting.com
Printed in the USA
LVHW05s0523010618
579193LV00006B/52/P